THE LONDON ENGLISH LITERATURE SERIES

General Editor: G. C. ROSSER M.A.

THE POETRY OF WORDSWORTH

THE POETRY OF WORDSWORTH

Selected and edited by

T. CREHAN M.A.

HODDER AND STOUGHTON
LONDON SYDNEY AUCKLAND TORONTO

ISBN 0 340 08362 X Paperback

First published in this edition 1965
Fourth impression 1978

Printed in Great Britain for Hodder and Stoughton Educational,
a division of Hodder & Stoughton Ltd.,
Mill Road, Dunton Green, Sevenoaks, Kent, by
Fletcher & Son Limited, Norwich

FOREWORD

THERE are many ways of reading literature. We can dip into a novel to pass the time away, we can give ourselves to a writer to escape from boredom or the monotony of films and television, we can read plays, short stories, and poems simply because we have developed a habit and would not be without our weekly instalment of reading. We can also read to make ourselves more mature by living through the emotional experience of other minds in this or another country. But whichever attitude we adopt, there is always one element which keeps us fascinated in literature. That element is pleasure. We read because, generally speaking, we find it pleasurable to read, and the more pleasure we find in reading the more the activity becomes part of our daily lives.

What many of us have realized, of course, is that pleasure and understanding go hand in hand—the more we possess a book, the more we come to grips with its essence, the more satisfaction it gives us. The experience becomes more relevant, more urgent. However, there are some books which we suspect contain more pleasure than we are able to extract. Their spirit seems to elude us. But with some guidance, we feel, we could possess a novel or a play or a poem and retain its genius. With such assistance in mind the present series has been edited to bring before the reader an opinion which may serve as a starting-point for discussion and fuller understanding. Each volume has a commentary or introduction which endeavours to look at a piece of literature as living imaginative experience. In this respect, therefore, it may be reassuring to find that with someone else's guidance before us we begin to see with a new and deeper perception. Our sympathy has developed, the satisfaction becomes more lasting.

G. C. ROSSER

CONTENTS

FOREWORD   5

INTRODUCTION   9

SUGGESTIONS FOR FURTHER READING   57

BIOGRAPHICAL NOTE   59

POEMS

Margaret, or The Ruined Cottage (1795–7)   65
The Old Cumberland Beggar (1797)   80

LYRICAL BALLADS (1798)
Simon Lee the Old Huntsman   86
The Idiot Boy   89
Lines Composed a Few Miles Above Tintern Abbey   104
The Last of the Flock   109
Her Eyes Are Wild   113
The Complaint of a Forsaken Indian Woman   116
Nutting (1798)   119
There Was a Boy (1798)   121

LUCY POEMS (1799)
Strange Fits of Passion   123
She Dwelt Among the Untrodden Ways   124
I Travelled Among Unknown Men   124
Three Years She Grew   125
A Slumber Did My Spirit Seal   126
Ruth (1799)   127
Michael (1800)   136
Andrew Jones (1800)   150
The Affliction of Margaret (1801)   152
Resolution and Independence (1802)   155

SONNETS
   Composed Upon Westminster Bridge, September 3, 1802   160
   The World is Too Much With Us   161
   Nuns Fret Not   161
   It is a Beauteous Evening (1802)   161
   Surprised by Joy (1812)   162
   After-thought   162
   London, 1802   163
Alice Fell (1802)   163
To The Cuckoo (1802)   166
The Sailor's Mother (1802)   167
Written in March (1802)   168
Ode: Intimations of Immortality from Recollections of Early
   Childhood (1802–4)   169
Beggars (1802)   176
I Wandered Lonely as a Cloud (1804)   178
The Solitary Reaper (1805)   179
Elegiac Stanzas Suggested by a Picture of Peele Castle (1805)   180
Character of the Happy Warrior (1805)   183
Ode to Duty (1805)   186

THE PRELUDE (1798–1805)
   Childhood 1 (From Book I)   )   188
   Childhood 2 (From Book II)   195
   The Theme (From Book III)   203
   The Discharged Soldier (From Book IV)   204
   Crossing the Alps (From Book VI)   207
   The French Revolution 1 (From Book X)   210
   The French Revolution 2 (From Book X)   212
   Rejection of Reason (From Book X, 1805 Text)   215
   Nature's Strength (From Book XI, 1805 Text)   223
   The Imagination (From Book XIV)   229

NOTES   239

INDEX OF FIRST LINES   253

INTRODUCTION

IN 1787, at the age of seventeen, Wordsworth entered St. John's College, Cambridge. The fact is important enough in itself, but especially so since the date marks the commencement of his first poem of any real length, "An Evening Walk". He had been writing poetry since the age of fourteen but this, together with the poem "Descriptive Sketches", begun in 1791, the year when he took his degree, represents the serious aspiration of a young man who had already consciously dedicated himself to poetry. "Descriptive Sketches" was the fruit of a walking tour through France and Switzerland undertaken in the long vacation of 1790. These were the years when a young man fresh from college would ordinarily think about his career. Wordsworth avoided the subject. During the critical years after graduation he spent his time writing poetry and walking. In 1795 a legacy of £900 provided him with a good reason for ignoring the matter of a career. This year marks the true beginning of his real vocation, poetry.

Changes

"An Evening Walk", written in the style of Gray's "Elegy", contains obvious echoes of a young man's reading. Gray's influence is everywhere in evidence: the "whistling swain" "plods his ringing way", the "solemn curfew" tolls, and the "sobbing owl complains". There is an "interlunar cavern" taken from Milton.

"Descriptive Sketches" is equally derivative. If Wordsworth had written no more he would have figured in literary histories as a minor poet of the late eighteenth century. With a knowledge born of hindsight we can pick out significant features from the two poems. We find in "An Evening Walk" evidence of a countryman's eye for exact observation:

9

> ... the shepherd in the vale
> Directs his winding dog the cliffs to scale,
> That, barking, busy 'mid the glittering rocks,
> Hunts, where he points, the intercepted flocks.

The swan's "brown little-ones" are "nibbling the water lilies", the "desert stone-chat" is heard. Wordsworth anticipates a pleasantly observant line from his own later poem "Tintern Abbey" with "And curling from the trees the cottage smoke".

"Descriptive Sketches" shows the beginning of change, particularly in the longer sentences which do something towards breaking the tyranny of the end-stopped line, but is in no way remarkable, despite some felicitous images. There are signs in it of Wordsworth's awakening interest in human beings. His "Grison gypsey" is observed with a compassionate eye, even though by implication. But between 1789 and 1798 the change becomes a matter for wonder. Miss Helen Darbishire has conveniently illustrated one aspect of it by placing side by side,

> And shades of deep embattled clouds were seen
> Spotting the northern cliffs with lights between,

from "An Evening Walk" (1787–9) and:

> Oh Soul of Nature! excellent and fair!
> That didst rejoice with me, with whom I too
> Rejoiced through early youth, before the winds
> And powerful waters, and in lights and shades
> That marched and counter-marched about the hills
> In glorious apparition,

from the first sections of *The Prelude* written in 1799. The laboured image of 1787 has become the impassioned, imaginative utterance of great poetry. The other aspect of change concerns the treatment of human figures. The *Lyrical Ballads* of 1798 are penetrating studies of human feelings beside which the descriptions of people in the two early poems appear superficial and fragmentary. The change first shows itself in "Margaret, or The Ruined Cottage" begun in 1795 and finished

. in 1797, a poem in which observation and expression, together with a surprisingly large understanding of the human condition, touch heights of genius. Until 1808 or thereabouts Wordsworth maintains this level, but afterwards, except for occasional flashes (and he could write great lines until the day of his death), he declines into mediocrity. His reputation rests on the decade 1798 to 1808.

Three events helped to bring about the transformation of 1795. In 1791–2 Wordsworth visited France where he saw, at first hand, some of the events and most of the idealism of the French Revolution. His natural interest in people deepened into an impassioned feeling which owed something, no doubt, to his love for Annette Vallon by whom he had a daughter. The second event was that in 1795, after receiving a legacy of £900 from his friend Raisley Calvert, he settled in Race-down with his sister Dorothy. Her influence upon him began in that year. He learned to share her extraordinary sensitivity to nature and to people. She revealed to him many things he had hitherto taken for granted. We can see from her diary, a record of her daily life, published as *Journals*, that her senses were sharply attuned to nature and that she had a gift for putting down in words of beguiling simplicity clear, fresh images of what she perceived.

The third event was friendship with Coleridge, whom the Wordsworths met for the first time in September 1795. Coleridge's subtle mind and eloquent conversation stirred Wordsworth profoundly. His understanding penetrated to levels of human behaviour which must have come upon Wordsworth with a shock of discovery. He certainly increased Wordsworth's awareness of the play of human feeling. Above all he gave him self-confidence.

From their discussions arose the *Lyrical Ballads*. Published anonymously in 1798, these poems were an act of rebellion against what both poets believed to be falseness in contemporary poetry. Avoiding the classical forms beloved of the eighteenth century they imitated the simple ballads of the people. Instead of eighteenth-century poetic diction they used ordinary language, near enough to the language of real men and women. The result was, of course, an experiment, never again repeated, but it was also a new kind of poetry in which the true nature of human feelings was expressed and through which the human situation, perhaps for the first time since Shakespeare, stood revealed in all its peculiar pathos.

Coleridge wrote about man as a moral being, placing his theme in a supernatural setting (his contribution was "The Ancient Mariner"), Wordsworth about particular persons in their familiar, everyday world, people undergoing the stress of emotion. He wrote twenty-two of the twenty-three poems. One differed strikingly from the rest. Autobiographical, intense, above all personal, and written in blank verse of magnificent flexibility, this odd poem out is the mature Wordsworth whom we first encountered in "Margaret, or The Ruined Cottage". The poem is "Tintern Abbey". Moving easily and power-fully it speaks of the poet's own inner life, unlike his other contributions to the *Lyrical Ballads* (indeed, "Tintern Abbey" is in no sense a ballad) in which the poet adopts the voice of a chosen subject—a mother, for instance, or a shepherd. Once established, the voice of "Tintern Abbey" sounds unmistakably through Wordsworth's best years, through the "Immortality Ode" and *The Prelude*. It is interest-ing to distinguish it from the voice of other poems in the great decade. The difference between the two voices represents Wordsworth's final step in the transformation dimly foreshadowed by the occasional felicities of "An Evening Walk" and "Descriptive Sketches".

A comparison of one of the *Lyrical Ballads*, "Simon Lee" (1798) with "Resolution and Independence" (1802), two poems with a similar subject, will make the difference clear. Wordsworth presents Simon in his *Lyrical Ballads* manner, that is to say, with a kind of dispassionate involvement. He notes aspects of Simon's appearance, the patched coat, the swollen ankles, but as an observer would note them, not as one concerned because of Simon's impact on his personal life. On the other hand, the leechgatherer in "Resolution and Independence" is related directly to Wordsworth's personal life; he is to the poet an example of endurance even more than he is a feature of the landscape, though he is both, and he is both because essentially he is an extension of Wordsworth himself. The poet sees the leechgatherer in a strongly subjective way. Similarly, "Lucy Gray" (1799) is a more or less ob-jective statement of a child's peculiar solitude, whereas "The Solitary Reaper" (1805) is a record of the poet's personal experience. Almost paradoxically, the leechgatherer and the reaper come before us the more vividly and convincingly for being presented in uncompromising subjective terms. The talented young imitator of 1787 has, indeed, become transformed.

Wordsworth's Private World

ONE of the most striking things about Wordsworth is his egocentricity. He talks at great length about himself—indeed, there are fourteen books on the subject, *The Prelude*. Sometimes he describes his own simple childhood experiences in a vivid and memorable way, some-times he makes extended statements about the nature of his mind at this or that stage of his life, and sometimes he applies general con-clusions, deduced from his own highly personal experience, to all mankind.

This last practice can be a source of confusion to the reader. The "Immortality Ode" (composed 1802 and 1804) opens with four stanzas of unmistakable personal statement, continues with four stanzas of assertion about the nature of birth, childhood, and growth (all, apparently, relating to mankind in general), and ends with three stanzas of further personal statement thinly and rather confusingly generalized by the use of the first person plural ("our embers", "We will grieve not"). Although the reader has no real difficulty in finding his way about the poem by separating general from particular, the fact remains that Wordsworth allows the one to run into the other. The child addressed in stanza VIII is child, Wordsworth, and man in general; the yoke bears down upon all three, all three come from the "imperial palace". The "primal sympathy", the "soothing thoughts", and "the faith that looks through death" are at once personal compen-sations to the poet for his loss of the "visionary gleam", lamented in stanzas I and II, and blessed gifts for all men to enjoy. Wordsworth sees, with double vision, mankind in himself and himself in mankind. Whatever confusion there is arises neither from the dualism nor from the vision but from the presentation, and the presentation takes for granted the reader's involvement in the poet's private world.

Explicit references to this world occur frequently in the poetry. Two in particular from prose sources, make the matter plain. The first is from the *Diary* of Joseph Farington who reports that:

> He (Wordsworth) told Constable that while he was a boy going to Hawkshead School, his mind was often so possessed with images, so lost in extraordinary conceptions, that he was held by a wall not knowing but he was part of it.

The second is the poet's frequently quoted note to Miss Isabella Fenwick, referring to his childhood:

> I used to brood over the stories of Enoch and Elijah, and almost to persuade myself that, whatever might become of others, I should be translated in something of the same way to heaven. With a feeling congenial to this, I was often unable to think of external things as having external existence, and I communed with all that I saw as something not apart from, but inherent in, my own immaterial nature. Many times while going to school have I grasped at a wall or tree to recall myself from this abyss of idealism to the reality.

Wordsworth's sense of lost identity seems to have been the pre-condition of a much more significant experience. He describes this experience in "Tintern Abbey" (1798) as a "blessed mood",

> In which the burthen of the mystery,
> In which the heavy and the weary weight
> Of all this unintelligible world,
> Is lightened—that serene and blessed mood,
> In which the affections gently lead us on—
> Until, the breath of this corporeal frame
> And even the motion of our human blood
> Almost suspended, we are laid asleep
> In body, and become a living soul:
> While with an eye made quiet by the power
> Of harmony, and the deep power of joy,
> We see into the life of things.

In other words the poet seems to see through sense-impressions into a transcendent reality, losing, in the process, his feeling of being him-

self, but gaining a joyful gift of deeper, larger, more meaningful existence. This gift, he feels, holds the key to our "unintelligible world".
The loss of identity is not complete, however: he becomes "a living
soul" and sees "into the life of things". His identity is changed rather
than lost though it is very different from the workaday self he takes
for granted. Other evidence, mainly from *The Prelude*, enables us to
reconstruct the experience fairly explicitly. The "visionary power" or
"plastic power", as Wordsworth calls it, is the heightened perception
that comes to him as he looks at a flower or a tree or some other object
in the countryside. An "auxiliar light" flows from his mind and bestows "new splendour" upon the object (*Prelude*, II, 368–70) which
then loses its identity and becomes a presence, or an energy, or a force.
This force, he believes, "impels all thinking things" as well as "all
objects of all thought". It is ubiquitous, pervasive, and cosmic. He
refers to it in "Tintern Abbey" as "a motion and a spirit", and in the
"Immortality Ode" he represents it as an "imperial palace" and an
"ocean".

Some scholars have either ignored, rejected, or under-estimated all
this. They have described Wordsworth's "visionary power", his sense
of transcendent reality, as manifestations of primitive animism such
as children and savages are supposed to experience. No doubt his boyhood feelings of being watched as he played among the hills, his sense
of a presence moving and breathing, can be attributed to some primitive impulse arising from fear, perhaps, and resembling what psycho-
logists describe as animism, but the sense of lost identity, the perception, and the exalted state of mind are different matters. Such features
have been observed in the experiences of men and women who are
freely acknowledged to be mystics. There is no reason why Wordsworth should be denied the description. Evelyn Underhill, a standard
authority on mysticism, might be describing Wordsworth in the statement that there are "three main types of experience which appear
again and again in the history of mysticism. . . . The actual physical
perceptions seem to be strangely heightened so that the self perceives
an added significance and reality in all natural things"; secondly, there
is a "joyous apprehension of the Absolute"; and thirdly, a capacity
for enormous increase in the energy of the power of perception.

Wordsworth apprehends the cosmic energy in a flash of illumination (mystics describe the process as the Illuminative Way) and is filled with joy in discovering, as he supposes, the source of all life. His senses sharpen during this experience, especially his sense of hearing: even the voice of the cuckoo leads him into the visionary world.

In *The Prelude* Wordsworth gives a thoroughgoing account of his mystic perceptions. Looking back to his childhood he regards the escapades of that time as a series of stepping-stones leading to the great visionary moments. His theft of the captured bird, for example, heightens his auditory sense to a point where he hears "low breathings" coming after him in the solitary hills; similarly, his feelings in the stolen boat, triggered off by a common or garden sense of guilt, are brought to an uneasy perception of a presence behind or implicit in the "grim shape" of Helvellyn. Both experiences begin in fear and end in awe, and both involve beautiful as well as frightening aspects of nature. Looking back upon such experiences, Wordsworth recognizes that beauty and fear, working on his mind through the forms of nature, have played a part of cardinal importance in his development:

> Fair seed-time had my soul, and I grew up
> Fostered alike by beauty and by fear.
>
> (*Prelude*, I, 301–2)

He refers in "Tintern Abbey" to this "seed-time" as a period of his youth, now passed, when "nature was all in all", that is, when the sights and sounds of the countryside produced in him a state of "dizzy rapture" without revealing, except by way of preliminary intimation, the cosmic energy:

> . . . The sounding cataract
> Haunted me like a passion: the tall rock,
> The mountain, and the deep and gloomy wood,
> Their colours and their forms, were then to me
> An appetite; a feeling and a love,
> That had no need of a remoter charm,
> By thought supplied, nor any interest
> Unborrowed from the eye.

In retrospect, the poet regards this condition of high excitement as an ecstatic prelude to the mystic event. Rather too readily, he attributes the condition to Dorothy, seeing in her his own youthful ardours:

> . . . in thy voice I catch
> The language of my former heart, and read
> My former pleasures in the shooting lights
> Of thy wild eyes.

He supposes his own personal experience of the cosmic energy to be exclusive and all powerful; Dorothy is shut out from it, cut off in the ante-room to the full mystic knowledge. In "Ruth" (composed 1799) Wordsworth attributes the same condition to his Georgian youth and adds the notion that the time of "dizzy rapture" can be attended by moral instability. The youth lives for the moment, marries Ruth in a fleeting mood of high ecstasy, which they both share and which has encouragement from nature, and deserts her when the mood dies. The time of "dizzy rapture" can therefore be dangerous when no clear moral direction is given it. The youth wooed the maiden with un-feigned delight, he responded to nature's beauties with some nobility of feeling, but he had lived with evil men and had become morally tainted: the high excitement produced by nature merely fed his selfish impetuosity.

Love

CLEAR moral direction came to Wordsworth from the cosmic energy itself. The light of the perceptive moment revealed it to him as the source of all matter, including life and the "mind of man", and as good. He had no need, therefore, to engage in exercises in moral philosophy to determine the nature of good: his knowledge of good came directly and new-minted from the visionary perception. The cosmic energy seemed to stand before him endowed with qualities about which there could be no argument. These qualities were unity, harmony, and a deep tranquillity. He believed completely in their existence and in their innate goodness, almost as God believed in the goodness of His creation: "And God saw every thing that he had made, and, behold, it was very good." Such qualities in men or between man and man argued the proximity of the cosmic energy. Love, then, Wordsworth supposed, must be the supreme human virtue, since it reflects most closely the attributes of the cosmic energy. The correspondence between love and the cosmic energy is axiomatic to Wordsworth; quite often he seems to think of love (in his Platonic moments) as an instrument of the cosmic energy.

He certainly regards it as the basis of all good society. Writing to Charles James Fox (14 January 1801), he asserts that the "domestic affections" must at all costs be protected from the depredations of poverty and the ill-effects of the rising tide of industrial development:

> . . . recently by the spreading of manufactures through every part of the country, by the heavy taxes upon postage, by workhouses, Houses of Industry, and the invention of Soup-shops etc, superadded to the increasing disproportion between the price of labour and that of the necessaries of life, the bonds of domestic feeling among the poor, as far as the influence of these things has extended, have been weakened, and in innumerable instances entirely destroyed.

In the same letter he extols the "small independent proprietors of land" in the Lake District as men who possessed strong affections for the land they owned and worked, and who, accordingly, were some of society's most valuable members. To this group belongs Michael who, rather than lose what is his, sends his son Luke to the distant city. Michael's world consists of land, cottage, independence, and, above all, love for wife, son, hearth, and home. His life is based upon love. The sheepfold built by father and son expresses and exercises the love between them. It possesses a function analogous to that of the Cumberland beggar, in the poem of that name, who exercises love in the hearts of the peasantry by acting as the object of their daily charity. Stimulated by such feelings, the peasantry represent, for Wordsworth, the best in English society. Their attachment to the soil, their powerful sense of community, their "domestic affections", are the foundations of true patriotism. They represented the England that Wordsworth would, if called upon, have fought for against Napoleon.

Evil, Suffering, and Love

LOVE of things, in its simplest form, is illustrated by the ballad of "Alice Fell". The little girl's love flows out upon her own particular cloak and no other. Love of persons, in its simplest form, stands revealed in "We Are Seven", where the child's love for her brothers and sisters excludes and therefore transcends the idea of death. Neither child can picture the irretrievable loss of what she loves because the universe she accepts unquestioningly is centred upon love: but Wordsworth was keenly and painfully aware that this same universe contained evil and suffering.

Perhaps the most vivid, certainly the most direct, illustration of what he considered evil was Andrew Jones in the poem of that name. Andrew's act is to steal two halfpennies from a helpless cripple. This, in Wordsworth's view, is deplorable because it expresses what is hostile to the virtue of the cosmic energy, for what is in direct opposition to kindness and love; it expresses cruelty and selfishness, disruptive forces dangerous to the sound health of a community. A man capable of such an act will certainly "breed his children up to pillage". Similar is "Peter Bell", but in his case Wordsworth emphasizes an important difference. Peter is a hard and selfish man, at first entirely immune to the great vehicle of the cosmic energy, nature.

> A primrose by a river's brim
> A yellow primrose was to him,
> And it was nothing more.

To some extent, Peter is fixed, like the Georgian youth, in the condition of "dizzy rapture":

> To all the unshaped half-human thoughts
> Which solitary Nature feeds
> 'Mid summer storms or winter's ice,
> Had Peter joined whatever vice
> The cruel city breeds.

We may suppose that nature produces in him something of the youth's feelings, but in general nature's effects are dangerous for the same

reason as they are dangerous in the youth, whose heartless act of desertion resulted from powerful, unstable feelings, encouraged by the
stimuli of nature's forms, but lacking moral direction. Peter Bell is
selfish and therefore evil, but the shock of discovering the body of a
drowned man and the demonstration of the donkey's fidelity to his
dead master change him. When he confronts the dead man's widow
in her grief, the transformation is certain; his mind is pervaded by a
sense of holiness, his heart opens. Unlike Andrew Jones, hardened in
selfishness, Peter is accessible to the influence of love. The evil in him
therefore yields.

In his unredeemed state Peter, like Andrew, caused suffering, as we
plainly see from his savage beating of the donkey. The question of
suffering touched Wordsworth closely. His first important poem on
the subject is "Margaret, or The Ruined Cottage", begun in 1795 and
finished in 1797, afterwards merged into Book I of "The Excursion".
In this extended account of a countrywoman's tribulations the poet
presents that combination of malignant circumstance and selfish behaviour which is so often the burden we have to bear. Margaret
carries her burden to the grave, enduring desertion by her husband
(whose selfishness in this respect has some small justification in the
poverty and idleness forced upon him by social changes over which he
can have no control), the death of her child, grinding poverty, and the
remorseless deterioration of her poor little thatched cottage. She never
loses the hope of her husband's return. She remains in the conjugal
home, even though it falls about her, loving it to the end. Her suffering finds no relief. The days add to her pain. Death alone brings peace;
and yet her spirit endures, unbroken. We are told:

> . . . that consolation springs,
> From sources deeper far than deepest pain,
> For the meek Sufferer,

and that the spear-grass on the wall, silvered over with mist and rain-
drops, conveyed to the Wanderer, who narrates the story, "an image
of tranquillity" which seemed to him to have power to assuage suffering. The deep sources of consolation lie in nature and the cosmic energy
for those able to profit from them. Such a one is Margaret. Her great

capacity for love and her "steady mind" enable her to receive the
soothing effects of nature's tranquil images and to acquire moral
strength. Her love is constantly renewed by daily contact with her
home and with the familiar sights and sounds of the countryside
around. She never despairs. The poet presents this bleak and wretched
life as a victory over suffering in which the human spirit preserves to
the end its moral integrity.

"The Complaint of a Forsaken Indian Woman" is little more than
the despairing cry of one left behind by the tribe to die and yet here,
too, the power of love is implied, in the woman's words:

> My poor forsaken Child, if I
> For once could have thee close to me,
> With happy heart I then would die.

The mad mother in "Her Eyes Are Wild" retains some sanity as long
as she has the love of the child at her breast; conversely, in "The
Affliction of Margaret", the loss of the child is presented as one of the
most acute because most exclusive forms of suffering:

> Beyond participation lie
> My troubles, and beyond relief.

Where a person's character is sound, as in "Margaret, or The Ruined
Cottage", love can help produce a victory over suffering; but it must
have an object and where the loved one is dead may transfer itself to
his possessions or to something connected with him. In "The Sailor's
Mother" the mother travels many weary miles to find,

> If aught which he had owned might still remain for me,

until she acquires his bird in its cage, and this becomes her consolation.
In "Michael", Michael's sheepfold serves a similar purpose. Here
Wordsworth states more explicitly than elsewhere his belief in the
power of love to overcome suffering. Michael's love for the countryside and his workaday association with the sheepfold he and his son had
built, assuage his grief:

> There is a comfort in the strength of love;
> 'Twill make a thing endurable, which else
> Would overset the brain, or break the heart.

The unsound character cannot win such victories. The shepherd in "The Last of the Flock" falls some way below Margaret and Michael because under a succession of heavy blows he breaks down. As his flock dies he becomes restless, his mind fills with "wicked fancies", he inclines to "wicked deeds", and he seems to love his children less. Margaret's husband belongs to the same class. The poet bestows upon him the virtues of sobriety, frugality and industry, but not a steady mind or a constant heart. Poverty crushes him. He speaks cruelly to his children, his joy in them becomes "false and unnatural", and in the end he deserts them. The weak or unstable succumb, losing the capacity for love and running to love's opposites: inconstancy, peevishness, and selfishness.

The time came for Wordsworth to wonder how he would himself face the kind of miseries he portrayed in his poems. He raises the question in "Resolution and Independence" and discovers some comfort in the leechgatherer's firmness of mind; but the question remained. Two special agonies awaited him: the loss of his cherished gift of the visionary power and the death by drowning of his beloved brother John. Both events lie at the heart of the "Immortality Ode". John Wordsworth perished with a large part of his crew when the ship he captained, the *Earl of Abergavenny*, sank off Weymouth in February 1805. The bereaved brother at first appeared inconsolable. He wrote to Sir George Beaumont:

> I trust in God that I shall not want fortitude; but my loss is great and irreparable. . . .

In other letters he returned again and again to the character of his lost brother, describing his modesty, his self-command, his taste in music and poetry, his courage and self-sacrifice at the moment of crisis, his gentleness, his firmness, his self-denial, and his capacity for attracting deep affection; but he found comfort at last in the certainty of his own strength to endure. This personal victory is clearly set out in the

"Elegiac Stanzas Suggested by a Picture of Peele Castle" where he welcomes

> . . . fortitude, and patient cheer,
> And frequent sights of what is to be borne!

and sounds a firm note of tempered optimism:

> Not without hope we suffer and we mourn.

Two other poems written in 1805, after John's tragic death, throw light on Wordsworth's attitude to suffering. The "Character of the Happy Warrior", composed to mark the death of Nelson but including sentiments connected with John Wordsworth, expresses the view of suffering as a training ground for character. The Happy Warrior is

> . . . more able to endure,
> As more exposed to suffering and distress.

The poem becomes essentially an analytic catalogue of virtues presented as precepts. The Warrior tries always to achieve good ends by good means (unlike Dion, in the poem of that name, whose death is a direct result of using bad means), seeking "good on good to fix". His actions are presented as emanations of character, but are also held up as guides to human conduct in general. In the "Ode to Duty", Wordsworth asks for the aid of rules of conduct: he needs not simply love and a free spirit, but clear precepts by which to live.

The question of suffering as he had personally experienced it can be fully understood only by reference to his loss of the visionary power. He had lost the power by 1802 (he laments its loss in the first four stanzas of the "Immortality Ode" written in that year). In 1805, the "visionary gleam" might well have sustained him through bereavement. Although he finds consolation in the memory of the power and in the continuing faith it has left him he needs compensation for the loss of the continuous renewal of optimism which visionary experience gave. Recollection is not enough, though it is something. He turns for this compensation, as we see in the "Character of the Happy Warrior", the "Ode to Duty", and in stanza X of the "Immortality Ode", to moral precepts. From 1805 onwards his faith rests less upon his diminishing memories of mystic events, and progressively more and more upon rules of conduct based upon such virtues as self-discipline, self-denial, and single-mindedness.

The Child as Father of the Man

WHEN, in the "Immortality Ode", Wordsworth speaks of

> . . . the soothing thoughts that spring
> Out of human suffering,

he declares his confidence in his own power to carry a personal cross as well as his belief that most men have the strength to endure and to avoid the paths that lead to moral breakdown. He places his view of suffering firmly against a general view of the universe and of human life set out clearly in the "Immortality Ode" and in "Tintern Abbey". "Tintern Abbey" belongs to 1798, the Ode, as we have seen, to 1802 and 1804. This is virtually the period covered by *The Prelude* (1796–1805), the main expression of Wordsworth's most cherished attitudes and beliefs.

In "Tintern Abbey" the poet relates how his youthful raptures, occasioned by the forms and sounds of nature, have given way to the "blessed mood", that is, to the visionary power. He talks of the strength he gains from the power, how it enables him to endure the "dreary intercourse of daily life" and to prevail against unkindness and selfishness in men. He asserts that his direct contact with the cosmic energy illumines for him man's nature. When in the full flood of vision the flower or the tree brightens, and all at once ceases to exist as a material form so that he "sees into the life of things", he becomes aware of man's spirituality. This awareness, he believes, visits many men, not through mystic experience, but through love, or kindness, or some kindred feeling, and it enables them to face hardship and generally to overcome it. When Wordsworth speaks of "the still, sad music of humanity" which "chastens and subdues" he refers to the inner strength of the human spirit.

The "Immortality Ode" develops the idea of man's soul or spirit into a more general hypothesis. As we have seen, the poem begins with an elegiac lament for the poet's loss of visionary power and ends with a list of compensations for the loss. Stanzas V to VIII present the theory of a pre-natal state, in which the human being's identity is merged into that of the cosmic energy though retaining a sense of separateness. Birth is detachment from the cosmic energy and therefore a kind of "sleep and a forgetting"; "God" in stanza V, "imperial palace" in stanza VI, and "immortal sea" in stanza IX all refer to the cosmic energy.

The "forgetting" is not complete. Wordsworth describes in *The Prelude* (II, 233–60), how the baby, with his soul "Drinks in the feelings of his mother's eye", that is to say, how he responds with his soul (recently part of the cosmic energy) to his mother's love. Wordsworth then assumes that, as the child's senses develop, his capacity for love grows by exercising itself upon a range of objects outside the mother, though she remains the centre of his universe. In the light of what the Ode tells us the following lines from this part of *The Prelude* acquire a new significance:

> No outcast he [the child], bewildered and depressed:
> Along his infant veins are interfused
> The gravitation and the filial bond
> Of nature that connect him with the world.
>
> (*Prelude*, II, 241–4)

The child is no outcast from the cosmic energy because love ("the filial bond") leads back to that source of life. Wordsworth speaks of love, in the rest of the passage, as if it shares, with his own visionary power, the ability to "irradiate and exalt". The child sees the flower, loves it, and at once adorns it with beauty. This capacity has to do, Wordsworth argues in another context, with imagination.

Returning to the Ode, we see that the child remembers his origin through love and so trails "clouds of glory"; but as he grows into adulthood, the business of life—marriage, death, "custom", as Wordsworth describes habits of life formed by repeating daily the necessary tasks connected with making a living, dulls and eventually suffocates and destroys the memory. In so far, therefore, as the child is near his

origin and exercises love as a creative, unifying and exalting function
he is wiser than the man whose daily routine has destroyed his recollection of the cosmic energy. Since the cosmic energy is the basis of
Wordsworth's faith in man's origin and end, the foundation of his
belief in the human power to overcome suffering, and the touchstone
of his morality, the child, being near it, becomes a "mighty prophet",
a "seer blest", a repository of truths which men toil to find, toil "in
darkness" because using not the babe's unhampered perception of
reality but the lesser gift of reason.

It is perhaps idle to speculate how many men Wordsworth includes
in this rather pessimistic conception of adulthood; obviously Andrew
Jones will belong to the category, and obviously all men do so in their
selfish moments. He believes that, in general, adulthood is a decline,
but for his own part it represents a change from the excitement of
mystical perception to the rather dull, if consoling, commonplaces of
a latter-day stoicism. The view expressed by some critics that Wordsworth's notion of the pre-natal state as a "sea" or "imperial palace" is
a myth through which he expresses his lost sense of the spirit of nature,
and that the Ode is particularly interesting as the only instance of his
use of such a technique, remains valid on condition that we do not
accept it as the whole explanation. It is immaterial whether or not the
poet really believed in a "sea" or a "palace" as long as we remain in
no doubt that he believed in a cosmic energy because he had experienced it. More serious is the view that what has been described as
mystic perception is no more than primitive animism refined into
pantheism. *The Prelude*, apart from other poems, contains too many
references of an unmistakable kind. No primitive animism explains
what happens to the poet when, as he says,

> . . . the light of sense
> Goes out, but with a flash that has revealed
> The invisible world.

(Prelude, VI, 600–2)

The sense of loss described in the "Immortality Ode" bears the mark
of an anguished interior monologue intended for the poet alone: it
is ludicrous to think of this agonized deprivation as the comparatively

mild emotion of one who no longer feels the presence of a supra-
human power in the hills, the lakes and rocks, the trees and flowers, of
his beloved native land.

Verse Texture: Unity

THE mystery of Wordsworth's decline as a poet which became painfully clear after 1808 is less intriguing than the miracle of his emergence
into greatness in the year 1795. We have already noticed a little of the
quality of the verse in "Tintern Abbey" (1798) as compared with the
poems of his youth, "An Evening Walk" and "Descriptive Sketches".
A mere eight years or so separates these from "Tintern Abbey", but
the difference in verse texture is astounding. "Descriptive Sketches"
dealt with roughly the same subject matter as Book VI of *The Prelude*,
when Wordsworth's powers were certainly at their highest pitch, and
some thirteen years separates them (Book VI was written in March
1804). In the famous passage from Book VI describing how Robert
Jones and Wordsworth crossed the Alps we can appreciate particularly
well his gift for combining description, narrative, exposition, sug-
gestive thrusts at deep though indefinable truths, and dramatic effect
achieved almost by stealth. Above all, we can see how the verse has
become the talking voice of the poet, easily and flexibly adapting itself
to the pitch and tone of his thought, moving continuously with inner
life, tightening and expanding, crystallizing and dissolving, yet never
breaking the proper discipline of the five-stressed line.

Informed with subjective colour from the poet's eye, the Alpine
scenes unfold before him as if in a voyage of discovery. Mont Blanc
itself disappoints him and perfectly adapting themselves to this mood
the lines run naked and lifeless to a dispirited halt:

> That very day,
> From a bare ridge we also first beheld
> Unveiled the summit of Mont Blanc, and grieved
> To have a soulless image on the eye
> That had usurped upon a living thought
> That never more could be.
>
> (*Prelude*, VI, 523–8)

But the halt is a mere pause in the onward thrust of the verse, which now fans out into a dream-like picture of Chamouny, a picture dissolving into movement as the poet speaks of the birds warbling and the eagle soaring, the movement gathering force like a descending boulder until we reach the image of Winter "making sport" among the cottages. As if to contain this movement, but, paradoxically, expressing it all the more effectively, the lines quite suddenly become end-stopped:

> There small birds warble from the leafy trees,
> The eagle soars high in the element,
> There doth the reaper bind the yellow sheaf,
> The maiden spread the haycock in the sun.
>
> (*Prelude*, VI, 534–7)

After the image of Winter follow lines of commentary catching exactly the tone of conversation, intimate and revealing (this kind of thing in later and inferior Wordsworth is simply heavy-handed moralizing). He speaks of the sweet, self-induced dejection of youth, placing it in contrast to the "stern mood" that seeks challenge. Fifteen lines of this prepare us for the resumption of the narrative. The long haul up the Simplon is perfectly evoked:

> When from the Vallais we had turned, and clomb
> Along the Simplon's steep and rugged road,
> Following a band of muleteers, we reached
> A halting-place, where all together took
> Their noon-tide meal.
>
> (*Prelude*, VI, 562–6)

Then comes the moment of real dejection, "a different sadness" arising from an "under-thirst of vigour", expressed in words of simple dramatic force:

> . . . *we had crossed the Alps.*

The statement gains power from the preceding lines of narrative. From the evocative passage of toilsome effort the language changes into a mood of spirited youthful aspiration:

> Hastily rose our guide,
> Leaving us at the board; awhile we lingered,
> Then paced the beaten downward way that led
> Right to a rough stream's edge, and there broke off;
> The only track now visible was one
> That from the torrent's further brink held forth
> Conspicuous invitation to ascend
> A lofty mountain.
>
> (*Prelude*, VI, 566–73)

They ascend but fail to overtake those who have gone ahead. The verse conveys an effect of rudderless motion as their doubts deepen into bewilderment:

> While every moment added doubt to doubt,
> A peasant met us, from whose mouth we learned
> That to the spot which had perplexed us first
> We must descend.
>
> (*Prelude*, VI, 578–81)

The truth, that they have achieved the crossing with ridiculous ease, comes over them in a wave of dismay. Returning to the mood of conversation the verse rapidly shifts into a strain of high seriousness, with unmistakable biblical undertones:

> Our destiny, our being's heart and home,
> Is with infinitude, and only there;

then spreads nobly, like a great estuary, in words comparing the soul to:

> . . . the mighty flood of Nile
> Poured from his fount of Abyssinian clouds.

Dismissed in two and a half lines of swift narrative, the episode gives way to a concluding passage of lyrical rhetoric in which description is made to feed an unrestrained forward thrust of the verse. An effect of accumulating power leads into lines of majestic and conclusive statement, a solemn assertion that the torrents, the rocks, and the "unfettered clouds" are:

> Characters of the great Apocalypse,
> The types and symbols of Eternity,
> Of first, and last, and midst, and without end.

After such splendour, we feel, what can possibly, let alone desirably, follow? What does follow illustrates a quality of poetic genius that lifts Wordsworth to a place among the immortals: a supremely easy return to narrative, in words of childlike simplicity, in phrases filled with afterglow of the great multiple theme of power, melancholy, and wonder. The young travellers find a night's lodging in a gloomy house, an unnecessarily large place, bombarded with the din of nearby waters. Sleep lies melancholy among their weary bones: we conjecture that the day's experiences are repeated to them during their disturbed rest rather as a coda repeats, retrospectively and less directly movingly, the themes of music. We are therefore carried back through the experience of the Alpine crossing by being told what happens at the end of that day. The effect finally achieved is to crystallize, or fix, events, so that they appear unique and wonderful.

As we read we are continuously aware of Wordsworth's sense of sound. In this, some of his best poetry, words become a range of finely-defined sounds, each precise in quantity and worth, acting singly or in concert, finding as if by a law of nature rhythmic patterns with or without the harmonizing influence of rhyme. The hand of the poet is concealed, the poem becomes an event, detached from its author. Such conventional tricks as metre, rhyme, and arrangement of lines are exalted by the plastic pervasive power of highly organized sound into something beyond themselves. A significant passage on sonnet-writing in a letter to Alexander Dyce (1833) shows how deeply conscious

Wordsworth was of the importance of sound in its relation to unity of effect. Writing about Milton's practice of allowing the meaning of the octave to run over into the sestet, he says:

> Now it has struck me, that this is not done merely to gratify the ear by variety and freedom of sound, but also to aid in giving that pervading sense of intense Unity in which the existence of the Sonnet has always seemed to me mainly to consist. Instead of looking at this composition as a piece of architecture, making a whole out of whole parts, I have been much in the habit of preferring the image of an orbicular body—a sphere—or a dew-drop.

The "pervading sense of intense Unity" of which he speaks here is by no means restricted to Milton's sonnets nor, indeed, to his own, nor is it a quality linked exclusively to sonority. "Tintern Abbey" possesses a remarkable unity of subject-matter. The "pastoral farms" set the opening scene and in the penultimate line they take on a new significance. The body of the poem falls into four sections in the sense Wordsworth speaks of, that is to say, four movements, like the movements of a sonata, or four spreading circles making a whole. Each movement is informed with energy. The poet *hears* the waters, *beholds* the cliffs, *connects* the landscape, and so on, and in the third movement he *bounds*. The second movement is linked to the first by the theme of the influence of the countryside upon the poet's mind. The second movement states the theme of mystic experience, or of an act of imagination in which "We see into the life of things"; the third returns to this theme almost in the manner of exposition; and the fourth speaks of the profound moral effect of nature upon character, an enlargement of the theme shared by the first and second movements. Wordsworth's ear for exact quantity and his gift for exalting simple words by placing them in uniquely appropriate patterns of sonority endow the poem with the unity of an "orbicular body". The simple word "five" becomes prophetic in:

> Five years have past; five summers, with the length
> Of five long winters! . . .

Each particular noun comes individually and singly before us: *waters, cliffs, sky, day, sycamore, plots.* At moments of intensity the particular stands out in bold, uncompromising relief:

> ... The sounding cataract
> Haunted me like a passion: the tall rock,
> The mountain, and the deep and gloomy wood,

and again, with rising ardour:

> ... the round ocean and the living air,
> And the blue sky, and in the mind of man.

The words are nothing in themselves. The adjectives are especially commonplace when taken out of context, very different from, say, the rich epithets of Keats (e.g. *purple-stained, freckl'd, vermilion-spotted*). And they would remain dead things if the poet were only the musician described above, with a musician's ear for pause, stress, and quantity. The life Wordsworth breathes into them comes ultimately from his own personal and urgent experience. For instance, the lines:

> ... Once again I see
> These hedge-rows, hardly hedge-rows, little lines
> Of sportive wood run wild ...

certainly owe much to the vivid concept of "sportive wood run wild" as well as to the keen ear for phrasing, but beyond these felicities stands intensity of vision. The entire poem is a personal revelation, an excited discovery, delivered from the poet to himself: we, the readers, merely listen in. There is a profound sense in which Wordsworth, despite his theory of the poet as a man speaking to men, speaks to himself alone. The paradox is that this poet of the people is a mandarin who makes us share his world. In the "Immortality Ode" we see the same skills at work as we see in "Tintern Abbey". In spite of the fact that the first four stanzas were written in 1802 and the remainder in 1804, and that there is a distinct break after stanza IV, the unity of the work is unmistakable. It is a unity of mood rather than of subject matter. The first two stanzas express simply and poignantly the mood of loss. Elevation of spirit occurs in stanza III, mounts rapidly throughout the stanza, the phrasing vigorous, even athletic, to the cry "I hear, I hear," of stanza IV, and all at once returns dramatically to the poem's initial mood. Stanzas V, VI, VII, and VIII take up once again the notion of loss, this time through the sorrowful concept of diminishing glory, until, at the end of stanza VIII, the nadir of gloom arrives with

Heavy as frost, and deep almost as life!

Again, as in stanza IV, there is a sudden and dramatic reversal, this time in stanza IX, with a cry of joy which echoes stanzas III and IV, but with the important difference that here the joy is reflective, aesthetically apt after the bitter almost Calvinistic gloom of stanzas V–VIII. Reflection and moralizing are easy bedfellows and Wordsworth's problem now is to avoid the leaden-footed effect of a reflection inclined away from liveliness. This he does by ringing the changes on thoughtful recollection of the visionary power and pure joy. Each of the last three stanzas begins in joy and ends in the measured dignity of tried and tempered faith. There is a particularly skilful return of the "imperial palace" of stanza VI at the end of stanza IX where it becomes an "immortal sea". The last verse maintains a mood of joyful, deeply grounded optimism almost unique in lyric poetry. The lost dream lamented in stanza I has become the moving conviction of:

To me the meanest flower that blows can give
Thoughts that do often lie too deep for tears.

Theory of Poetry—The Lyrical Ballads

How much Wordsworth's style owes to his theory of poetry is open to question. The theory is justly famed and still discussed. It appeared in 1800 as the Preface to his Lyrical Ballads (first published jointly with Coleridge in 1798) and again in 1802 when Wordsworth published an extensively revised and substantially enlarged version for the third edition of the Lyrical Ballads. Coleridge discussed the Lyrical Ballads and in particular the Preface in Chapters 14, 17, 18, 19, 20, and 22 of his Biographia Literaria. No study of the Preface is complete which fails to include this criticism.

B

It may well be true, as some scholars have asserted, that Words-worth's arguments suffer from a weakness in making distinctions, from an inability to qualify definitions, from ambiguities, but he leaves us in no doubt that he believes a poet's sacred duty is to communicate to as wide an audience as possible. From this belief comes his insistence that the poet is "a man speaking to men in the language of men" and his emphatic hostility to poetic diction, including, specifically, personification and hackneyed "poetic" phrases. He turns against the eighteenth-century idea of a poet as a chosen individual writing in a special hieratic language for a special audience of perceptive and educated persons capable of appreciating general statements of a more or less moral kind dressed up in flowing numbers.

In his *Lyrical Ballads* Wordsworth used a language essentially simple and clear, a kind of everyman's language, free, therefore, from regional variations and vulgarity. He chose "incidents and situations from common life", by which he meant "humble and rustic life", where, he argued, "the essential passions of the heart find a better soil in which they can attain their maturity". He used metre and rhyme on a number of grounds, but particularly because such devices prevent deep emotion from becoming unbearable to the reader and, conversely, raise the temperature of feeling where necessary.

The impact of these views upon men's minds in the early years of the nineteenth century was immense. The idea that a poet could and should write about ordinary matters seemed to imply that he could write about anything, certainly about subjects which were not necessarily to be chosen for their aptness in illustrating general principles. On the face of it, this theory was directly opposed to eighteenth-century standards. The poem of Betty Foy and her idiot boy, for instance, is exactly opposed to Imlac's precepts in Chapter X of Johnson's *Rasselas*, since it is about the "individual" not the "species" insofar as it concerns particular persons in a particular place and situation, and, even more, in a particular variant of the mother–son relationship: and yet, Johnson's general principle is manifestly evident because the story is so presented that the anxieties, the hopes, fears, and above all the love of Betty for her idiot son illustrate mother-love in general. Moreover, the reader's pleasure is enlarged by his awareness of the general in the particular, and by the balance of the parts: the story is interesting in itself, and yet subordinate to the feelings described—the display of mother-love is brought to a natural peak of intensity at the moment when Betty finds her son. The mother's feelings owe much of their depth to their being presented in a context of ordinary daily life heightened: Betty's neighbour Susan is desperately ill and only Betty can help, the family doctor is uncivil when called upon in the early hours, the familiar downs assume an ominous appearance after Betty's fearful discovery that Johnny has not even reached the doctor's house:

> She listens, but she cannot hear
> The foot of horse, the voice of man;
> The streams with softest sound are flowing,
> The grass you almost hear it growing,
> You hear it now, if e'er you can.

Such writing aptly illustrates Wordsworth's view of poetry as simple, natural language, speaking from the heart and finding a wide response. The *Lyrical Ballads* provide numerous examples of a similar kind. There are, of course, the failures, upon which perhaps too much emphasis has been placed, the passages in which simpleness passes for simplicity, the ridiculous for the moving, but these pale before the successes. It is interesting to note that the *Lyrical Ballads*, after a fairly modest start, made their way rapidly during the first decade of the nineteenth century, in spite of those who regarded them (amazing as it may seem to us now) as the productions of a country bumpkin.

Two features of the *Lyrical Ballads* and of other poems by Wordsworth in the same manner deserve special mention since they are characteristic of his skill as a ballad poet. The first can best be demonstrated by reference to the Lucy poems (which are not among the *Lyrical Ballads*). It is an effect of profound feeling produced by skating perilously near the ridiculous. The third verse of "She dwelt among the untrodden ways" ends:

> But she is in her grave, and, oh
> The difference to me!

a sigh from the heart's core owing much to its proximity to the bathetic. Dr. F. R. Leavis has most perceptively noted Wordsworth's gift for pathos/bathos in his appendix on the Lucy poem "Strange fits of passion" in *Revaluation*. The second feature is the marriage of narration to character and feeling. Despite obvious blemishes—downright silliness, childish phrasing, and so forth—there is scarcely a ballad by Wordsworth in which the place, the situation, and the person are not indissolubly linked. Simon the huntsman's lost strength comes before us in all its sadness because the incident of the tree, exactly appropriate to his daily life as a countryman, perfectly conveys his weakness, and because the cunning hand of the artist places the incident after the account of Simon's vigorous youth and subsequent decline in age, even after the poet's childish commentary:

> O gentle Reader! you would find
> A tale in every thing.

In brief, an old man's weakness is presented in its relationship to the whole vision of man's decline in age and sickness so that the poem's trite, moralizing conclusion is illuminated from within by the pathos of human life itself:

> —I've heard of hearts unkind, kind deeds
> With coldness still returning;
> Alas! the gratitude of men
> Hath oftener left me mourning.

Emotion Recollected in Tranquillity

WORDSWORTH's capacity for wholeness of vision may well stand behind his celebrated theory of the creative act of poetry. He writes perceptively and informatively about the act:

I have said that poetry is the spontaneous overflow of powerful feelings: it takes its origin from emotion recollected in tranquillity: the emotion is contemplated till, by a species of reaction, the tranquillity gradually disappears, and an emotion kindred to that which was before the subject of contemplation, is gradually produced, and does itself actually exist in the mind. In this mood successful composition generally begins, and in a mood similar to this is it carried on.

The process thus described, continues Wordsworth, is pleasant, and the poet's mind "will, upon the whole, be in a state of enjoyment". The recollection involves the poet in an act of imagination, not simply of remembering: he must re-create the emotion by identifying himself with it to the point where it becomes a real thing, existing, with a life of its own, in his mind. We are not to suppose, however, that the re-created emotion exists, by proxy, in all its original form. Wordsworth's idea is that the poet retains the original impression of what he originally perceived, that this impression cannot be a complete reproduction of the event but must be, in the nature of things, a version of it. Lying fallow in the poet's mind for a period of time, perhaps for years, the impression is called up and re-created; but the act of re-creation involves a selection from the material of the original impression, so that what becomes the substance of the poem is a sifted, selected version of an emotional event observed by the poet in past time. The modifications made to the original impression will occur from the moment of its birth in the perceiving mind, and will continue throughout the period of lying fallow in the mind as well as during the act of poetic creation itself. Imagination, a faculty of mind discussed and defined by both Wordsworth and Coleridge, seems to include, as far as Wordsworth is concerned, these selecting, remembering, and shaping functions (it is interesting to note that the word is never used in the Preface to *Lyrical Ballads*).

H. W. Garrod quotes Aubrey de Vere's record of a conversation with Wordsworth in which Wordsworth spoke of an inferior descriptive poet as one who did not understand the art of selection, certainly not as an art demanding reflection and recollection:

Nature does not allow an inventory to be made of her charms. He should have left his pencil behind, and gone forth in a meditative spirit; and *on a later day*, he should have embodied in verse, not all he had noted, but *what he best* remembered of the scene; and he would then have presented us *with its soul*, and not with the mere *visual aspects of it.*

This technique of watchful reflectiveness, of selection followed by imaginative creation, fits perfectly Wordsworth's predilection for specific objects and for solitary figures—soldiers, beggars, sturdy independent yeomen farmers, children, and so forth. It is convenient for him to recollect in tranquillity the emotion of, say, mother-love felt by one person, Betty Foy, for her son Johnny, since there are no complexities introduced by conflicting or attendant emotions expressed by other persons: the poet is able to fix his regard unswervingly upon the play of maternal feeling and to present it in varied aspects. In other words, the process of selection may not be so extensive and difficult as we may at first suppose although it would be quite wrong to assume that Wordsworth made it easy for himself by keeping to simple, uncomplicated subjects. He must still select those features of Betty's emotions which reveal the depth, pathos, and power of her motherhood.

"Margaret, or The Ruined Cottage" affords apt illustration of the power of selection operating through reflection and retrospection. The growing bitterness and despair of Margaret's husband is measured by the following specific instances: he stands at the door of his cottage whistling merry tunes—

> That had no mirth in them; or with his knife
> Carved uncouth figures on the heads of sticks—

he does odd jobs about the cottage, jobs belonging to all seasons; he wanders across the fields; he tosses his babies "with a false unnatural joy", and then disappears. The process of moral collapse under the weight of illness and poverty emerges with simple starkness through each specific action. Similarly, and even more movingly, Wordsworth chooses features of physical decay, from the yellow stone-crop growing unchecked along the window ledge, the red stains smeared by sheep on the corner-stones of the white porch, to the visible depredations made upon the very fabric of the cottage "by frost, and thaw, and rain".

Wordsworth's Solitaries

JUDGING from his *Letters* and from Dorothy's *Journals*, Wordsworth had frequent encounters with solitary figures—shepherds, sailors (the coast was near), beggars, wagoners, leechgatherers, small farmers, soldiers, and so forth. As we have seen, he admired the sturdy independence of the yeomen farmers, seeing in it the basis of true patriotism, and the power of the family as a solid unit and a source of "domestic affections". In the letter to Charles James Fox, already quoted (see page 18), he praises the "small independent proprietors . . . men of respectable education who daily labour on their own little properties", and declares that their "little tract of land serves as a kind of permanent rallying point for their domestic feelings, as a tablet upon which they are written which makes them objects of memory in a thousand instances when they would otherwise be forgotten".

The "independent proprietor" is most strikingly represented by Michael. When dispossession threatens, he is prepared to send away his only son, Luke, even at the cost of breaking up the family, so that the land shall remain and be handed down. Independence, as a quality in itself, is emphasized in the character of the leechgatherer in "Resolution and Independence" and in the character of Alice Fell, whose attachment to what is especially hers reveals a spirit owing nothing to anyone. Above the moral power of the one and the capacity for love of the other stands their strength as individual human beings. We may suppose the old Cumberland beggar a model of dependence, "a solitary man", "helpless in appearance", until we learn that his function is to exercise charity in the hearts of the villagers who have, for years, freely and generously bestowed alms upon him. Wordsworth's solitaries frequently possess two other characteristics, impressive appearance (not necessarily, though sometimes noble) and a natural gift of speech. For example, the leechgatherer's words follow each other "in solemn order",

> . . . a stately speech;
> Such as grave Livers do in Scotland use,

and although age has bent him double he impresses the poet as the oldest man he has ever seen. Again, the beggar woman in "Beggars" is made to resemble an Amazonian queen.

Wordsworth's solitaries are generally lonely figures, like the leech-gatherer or the Indian woman, though sometimes he singles them out for special attention, as the beggar woman or Michael. We must not suppose that he saw lonely or solitary figures where none existed, however; there are numerous references in Dorothy's *Journals* to such persons and there is no doubt that brother and sister shared an interest in them. Their interest was not quite of the same order, as we can see from comparing their reactions to the leechgatherer. We can compare the brother's poem on the subject with the sister's prose account. Her *Journal* entry, dated 3 October 1800, describes how she and William met the leechgatherer:

> When William and I returned from accompanying Jones, we met an old man almost double. He had on a coat, thrown over his shoulders, above his waistcoat and coat. Under this he carried a bundle, and had an apron on and a night-cap. His face was interesting. He had dark eyes and a long nose. He was of Scottish parents but had been born in the army. He had had a wife and "a good woman. and it pleased God to bless us with ten children". All these were dead but one, of whom he had not heard for many years, a sailor. His trade was to gather leeches, but now leeches are scarce, and he had not strength for it. He lived by begging, and was making his way to Carlisle, where he should buy a few godly books to sell. He said leeches were very scarce, partly owing to this dry season, but many years they have been scarce—he supposed it owing to their being much sought after, that they did not breed fast and were of slow growth. Leeches were formerly 2/6d per 100; they are now 30/-. He had been hurt in driving a cart, his leg broke, his body driven over, his skull fractured. He felt no pain till he recovered from his first insensibility. It was then late in the evening when the light was fast going awry.

Details of the man's appearance, of his personal history, even down to the price of leeches and the time of evening give Dorothy's picture a hard, memorable clarity: she refrains from comment, simply presenting the facts, but the overall effect is unmistakable. Two years later, in "Resolution and Independence", Wordsworth places this old man in a situation of obvious loneliness on the moor by a pond. He reduces circumstantial detail to an absolute minimum, the old man is still "bent double", he is said to appear neither alive nor dead, so extreme is his age, and his speech is stately. Apart from his notion of the leechgatherer as the symbol of endurance Wordsworth's essential view of him is presented in stanzas IX to XII. He is:

> Like a sea-beast crawled forth, that on a shelf
> Of rock or sand reposeth, there to sun itself.

Dorothy's lonely old man stripped of family and friends, is perfectly comprehensible to us as a poor, suffering beggar finding his livelihood where he can; Wordsworth transforms him into a kind of human outcropping of nature, standing somewhere between man and matter. His loneliness becomes deeply organic, the loneliness of a solitary whose life is nourished at the secret sources of nature and who needs no companion. What there is of circumstantial detail conveys much of suffering and hardship and brings him firmly into the human fold. The poet's general terms, "pain", "sickness", retain enough mystery and convey enough concrete fact to preserve firmly in our minds the vision of a solitary, human yet remote, man yet integral part of nature. It is a vision owing everything to the manner of its presentation: the leechgatherer is a statuesque figure, a "stone", a "sea-beast", a "cloud", who dissolves into dreamlike movement when he stirs the pond. This manner is sustained in the subsequent verses by the use of reportage, the effect of which is to keep the leechgatherer at arm's length, as a picture we can see clearly only at a proper distance. The moralizing is so gently and aptly introduced that we scarcely, at first, recognize it as comment. In the penultimate stanza Wordsworth withdraws into personal reflection (not comment), returning to his subject in the last stanza so that when it comes the comment seems to arise naturally from the subject:

> I could have laughed myself to scorn to find
> In that decrepit Man so firm a mind.

Wordsworth's idea of a solitary as standing somewhere between man and matter is aptly illustrated by the episode of the soldier in Book IV of *The Prelude*. In this case, however, we witness the emergence of the solitary, under the poet's hand, from the state of matter. Wordsworth comes upon him suddenly, at a bend in the road, motionless, statuesque. He is propped up against a milestone. Now the idea of a solitary includes that of observer: the solitary is one who is watched. Wordsworth immediately becomes the watcher:

> . . . slipping back into the shade
> Of a thick hawthorn, I could mark him well,
> Myself unseen. . . .
>
> (*Prelude*, IV, 389–91)

This is the starting point of the episode's development. At first the poet sees an "uncouth shape" take a vaguely human form in his perceiving eye. The shape acquires more specific and defined characteristics, lankness and meagreness, sustained, allusively, throughout the conversation that follows, until it becomes the soldier whom the poet questions. The answers are expressed in a "strange half-absence":

> . . . as of one
> Knowing too well the importance of his theme,
> But feeling it no longer.
>
> (*Prelude*, IV, 443–5)

Gradually but firmly the poet's compassion, implicit throughout the episode, establishes the lonely figure as human. When he parts from the poet, who has befriended him to the extent of finding him lodging, his words reveal "reviving interests". He has been brought back into the human fold. The initial situation of watcher and watched has been transformed into that of helpmate and sufferer: solitary and observer enter together into the brotherhood of man.

The fact that they do so shows how near they are to one another. They are, in fact, interchangeable. The Wanderer in *The Excursion* (from the early section composed in 1802) is Wordsworth himself, the observer turned observed (the introductory lines setting out his history are really a summary of extensive observation), and still the observer *par excellence*. From his vantage point of professional nomad, he can devote himself to the twin functions of solitary and observer. As an observer he is supreme: what he sees, he sees in a clear, unifying radiance. He stands before the personal saga of Margaret, influencing it, indeed, entering it, in no way whatever, yet comprehending it and conveying both its depth and its pathos. His is the humility of one standing before the essential tragedy of the human situation. His dismissive words imply the continuity of life:

> She sleeps in the calm earth, and peace is here.

The Wanderer is Wordsworth's ideal solitary in the sense that he is trained for the job. A rich spiritual education acquired from nature, and a wide acquaintance with suffering humanity, enable him to transcend self by acts of imaginative projection into the lives of people like Margaret.

Nature

WORDSWORTH'S solitaries are essentially alone with nature. The Wanderer's footsteps never take him to cities. We have seen how nature, in the sense of trees, rocks, hills, and so forth, kindled the poet's mind at an early age, and how what has been described as his mysticism arose from his particularly intense feelings about such things. Wordsworth's idea of nature is by no means simple and by no means single: he applies the word variously to human beings, rocks, transcendental power, immanent beauty (arising from the sound of water or the sight of flowers), and to the abstraction used by eighteenth-century writers. He can think of nature as a teacher, a guide, a frightening force, an influence for good, and an instrument of God. These multiple meanings cannot be parcelled up in the glib assertion that Wordsworth was a pantheist or an animist, though he was both.

He begins in the eighteenth century and ends in the nineteenth because he reflects the changing pattern of thought which emerged with the French Revolution. His first idea of nature differed little from the generally accepted eighteenth-century one. In "Descriptive

Sketches" he uses the word as an abstract term to denote laws or principles of the Universe, laid down by a wise Deity. This meaning is perfectly conventional for its time. The eighteenth century tended to view the Universe as a mathematical demonstration of the power of divine logic: all the parts fitted together and made sense to those whose reason enabled them to understand. Human nature was simply the supreme earthly demonstration of God's skill. At the same time, throughout the century and with gathering force in the last two decades, the idea that Nature (the great abstraction demanded the capital letter) was good and corrupted only by artificial arrangements, social, political and the like, found numerous advocates, from Rousseau to Mrs. Inchbald. Such advocacy helped powerfully to shape the forces that were to produce the French Revolution which, when it came, seemed "nothing out of Nature's course" to those who believed, with Rousseau, that Man is born free but everywhere is in chains.

In brief, Wordsworth grew up in an intellectual climate which extolled reason as revealed in the pattern of the Universe and as demonstrated in human beings, and which asserted that there was a natural human condition, existing before societies and states, in which Man was both free and good. So it was that, in common with many young, and not so young, men of his day, he welcomed the French Revolution as a clearing away of accumulated wrongs and a first step towards the return of Man to his primitive state of grace.

In Books IX, X, and XI of *The Prelude* he describes his experiences during the French Revolution. Besides the holiday tour made in 1790 to France and Switzerland with his friend Robert Jones, Wordsworth visited France from November 1791 to December 1792, and perhaps again in 1793. During the spring of 1792 he met Michel Beaupuy, a French Army captain who had seen enough of the miseries of the people to become an ardent revolutionary, and whose wide culture and acquaintance with political thought convinced him that the cause of revolution was just. Wordsworth's friendship with Beaupuy strengthened his conviction that the Revolution was just and inevitable; his deepest emotions were fully engaged on the side of the French people, not only because he believed that nature was asserting

herself through the revolutionary movement but also because he fell
in love with Annette Vallon.

These feelings received a series of profound shocks as, first, England
declared war on France (February 1793) and then the glorious promise
of revolution became submerged in the Terror. In *The Prelude* he
describes how he recoiled from the idea of supporting his native land
in her war against France, how the event was a heavy blow to his
"moral nature", and how he "exulted":

> Exulted, in the triumph of my soul,
> When Englishmen by thousands were o'erthrown,
> Left without glory on the field, or driven,
> Brave hearts! to shameful flight.
>
> (*Prelude*, X, 285-8)

His loyalties were deeply divided. He believed that if France prospered
the millennium could not be long delayed but that England had set
herself up as a bar to progress. And yet he noted disturbing signs. The
"domestic carnage" of the Terror made him forget, from time to
time,

> . . . that such a sound was ever heard
> As Liberty upon earth . . .
>
> (*Prelude*, X, 377-8)

In spite of Robespierre's worst actions, however, he refused to blame
the Revolution or its ideals, explaining the horror as "a terrific reservoir
of guilt" which had "burst and spread in deluge through the land".
Robespierre's death in 1794 renewed his hopes: he reiterated his trust
in the people of France, in his conviction that nature, that is, natural
goodness, would prevail. The final shock came when Revolutionary
France attacked her neighbours. Like many young radicals of the
twentieth century Wordsworth felt the bitterness of a shattered dream:

> But now, become oppressors in their turn,
> Frenchmen had changed a war of self-defence
> For one of conquest, losing sight of all
> Which they had struggled for . . .
>
> (*Prelude*, XI, 206-9)

Sometime towards the end of 1794 Wordsworth turned in upon himself and reviewed his most cherished beliefs. He held fast to the idea that man was naturally good and that human societies had become oppressive, but concluded that emotion had misled him into an inaccurate assessment of the obstacles to be overcome. It seemed to him now that Man could enter the state of nature only by achieving self-mastery, and self-mastery only through reason. Speaking retrospectively, he says of this time of intellectual and spiritual crisis that he was confounded by "outward accidents" and that his heart "had been turned aside from Nature's way". The turning aside of which he speaks is the turning to reason. For some months of 1795 he turned to mathematics for relief and to William Godwin for a new way. Godwin's teaching, as set forth in *Political Justice*, emphasized reason as the supreme intellectual faculty. Leaving feeling out of his reckoning Wordsworth tried to follow Godwin in accepting the view that nature meant the way of reason. He tested everything by reason,

> Dragging all precepts, judgments, maxims, creeds,
> Like culprits to the bar;
>
> (*Prelude*, XI, 294-5)

until he "lost all feeling of conviction" and, puzzled and exhausted by contradictions which reason seemed unable to resolve, he "yielded up moral questions in despair".

Wordsworth's recovery came in the summer of 1795 and is marked by his poetic play *The Borderers* (composed 1795-6). In this play he demonstrates how a man can follow the path of reason and still perform the most wicked actions, how, in fact, reason divorced from moral purpose is not only useless but dangerous. Retaining his republicanism, his humanitarianism (which he shared with Godwin), and his respect for reason—well this side idolatry—Wordsworth freed himself from the errors (as he supposed them) of Godwinism, established himself in Somerset with his sister Dorothy, and in her company re-discovered nature. She helped him to remember his childhood and to return to that nature which became for him Nature, the countryside. His meeting with Coleridge in 1795 and his subsequent stay at Alfoxden with Dorothy in 1797, prepared the way for the walks and

talks of all three out of which, as we have seen, the *Lyrical Ballads*
were to emerge. Coleridge's influence upon Wordsworth was con-
siderable. If Dorothy reopened his eyes to nature, Coleridge brought
him to an understanding of man as a many-sided being, not simply a
feeling animal in Rousseau's sense or a reasoning machine in Godwin's.
In the society of these two and the peace of the countryside Wordsworth looked upon nature and reflected upon men as individuals
compounded of feelings, instincts, and predispositions. For the
grandiose eighteenth-century abstractions, Man, and Nature, he sub-
stituted the concept of nature as the countryside, a combination of
physical features with power to influence and educate its human
occupants, and nature as the individual man or woman. In *The Prelude*, his greatest poem, he writes about the individual man he knew
best and most intimately, himself, and about the effect upon this man
of the country he knew best and most intimately, the Lake District.
The poem is an exploration of his own personal history, beginning in
childhood and proceeding with extended and penetrating accounts of
the influence upon him, as he grows and develops, of the hills, valleys,
rocks, and lakes of his native land. Nature means, throughout, the
poet's human nature, changing, developing, and, indissolubly linked
to this, the countryside: in a sense, each is an aspect of the same thing.
Wordsworth rarely thinks of the flower or the tree without including,
in his thought, a human being who may observe or be influenced by
the natural object. In that aspect of this concept we commonly call
nature he found the certainty and faith which, for a time, the latter
days of the French Revolution and the months of Godwinism had
obscured. In this nature he discovered "Authentic tidings of invisible
things", and

> . . . central peace, subsisting at the heart
> Of endless agitation,
>
> (*Excursion*, IV, 1146–7)

and his thoughts "flowed clear". Such discoveries led to the remarkable states produced in him by nature and described so vividly in *The
Prelude* when the invisible world was revealed to him.

What Wordsworth had sought in the French Revolution and

Godwinism he found in nature. Nature, he believed, was essentially good. It influenced the responsive individual in a moral direction and the responsive individual was generally a child or a peasant, one whose spirit was not crushed by custom or the accumulated actions of daily routine inside human society, especially such highly organized societies as those of the city. He did not turn against reason; on the contrary, he continued to regard it as one of the most precious faculties of the human mind. His deeper understanding of man and nature had, he believed, taught him that the faculty of mind responsible for his mystic perceptions must be given absolute pride of place since these perceptions had brought him mental peace and firm conviction.

Imagination

THE supreme faculty Wordsworth calls imagination is the faculty which, in the last book of *The Prelude*, he extols as "the feeding source" of his "long labour". Recapitulating what he has said about imagination in the poem, he describes, in the lines immediately preceding the reference to "the feeding source", how love has been quickened in him by nature's daily provision of "sublime or beautiful forms", and by experience of pain and joy and fear.

He exclaims:

> . . . By love subsists
> All lasting grandeur, by pervading love;
> That gone, we are as dust.
>
> (*Prelude*, XIV, 168–70)

As we have seen, his notion of love is tethered to the conviction that all love in a greater or lesser degree is an expression of the unifying force in the world we have called cosmic energy. The highest love, it follows, will stand nearest this transcendental source, and this he calls "spiritual Love" which, he asserts, cannot exist without imagination, imagination which

> Is but another name for absolute power
> And clearest insight, amplitude of mind,
> And Reason in her most exalted mood.
>
> (*Prelude*, XIV, 188–92)

Imagination includes the visionary power ("clearest insight") which is a particularly dramatic aspect of imagination's workings. In the passage in Book VI, describing his journey across the Alps with his friend Robert Jones, Wordsworth tells how imagination yields to the vision itself. Following the Simplon Pass, he expected and hoped and desired that there would be great obstacles to surmount: his imagination built up a picture of massive challenge when, all at once, he learned that he and his friend had quite easily and suddenly crossed the Alps. The incident, he reflects, illustrates how the event usurped what he had imagined: in the same way, he argues, imagination heightens with "auxiliar light" what the eye perceives, until "the light of sense goes out" and the "invisible world" stands revealed; until, in fact, imagination dies in vision, or in other language, achieves its fullest realization in the transcendental moment. Such clarity of perception he describes as

> . . . clearest insight, amplitude of mind,
> And Reason in her most exalted mood.

Wordsworth's identification of reason with imagination is not easy to understand. He certainly does not mean analytic reason. He uses the word to connote exactness of vision, to dispel any notion that what he perceives is vague, woolly, or visionary in the vulgar sense of that word. It is difficult to escape the feeling that he wants to present himself as he undoubtedly is, a practical down-to-earth man whose faculties, though higher in kind, are those of other men.

Wordsworth has much to say about imagination as it reveals itself in poetry: so, indeed, has Coleridge, and Shelley's *Defence of Poetry* rests the whole structure of its argument upon the thesis that poetry, like many human arts, is an expression of imagination (raised in our esteem by being spelt with a capital "I", as in Wordsworth and Coleridge). The youthful optimism and idealism, the independence of mind and respect for the free play of intellect, the conviction that man and the universe turn ultimately upon the principle of good, and that once artificiality, corruption, and restrictive institutions have been cleared away man will be able to breathe freely and reveal his natural goodness—all this Wordsworth carried over from the intellectual milieu of the French Revolution into the sphere of nature and poetry. Poetry, at least the best poetry, resulted, he believed, from the working of imagination, just as his "sense of something deeply interfused" in nature arose from the same faculty. He never forgets that imagination, operating in poetry or anywhere else, relies upon the senses, and on this he has much to say. We have already noticed how acute was his sense of hearing. He is aware that the senses (or even one particular sense) are capable of dominating the mind to the point of preventing the imagination from working. In Book XII of *The Prelude* (lines 127–31) he writes:

> I speak in recollection of a time
> When the bodily eye, in every stage of life
> The most despotic of our senses, gained
> Such strength in me as often held my mind
> In absolute dominion.

In his Preface to the 1815 edition of his poems, Wordsworth analyses, with striking illustration, imagination in poetry and goes on to distinguish it from fancy. He declares that the word denotes "operations of the mind upon . . . objects", that is to say, upon sense-impressions, and proceeds to illustrate how imagination endows, modifies, shapes, and creates. He thinks of it as a plastic power moulding sense-impressions into forms pregnant with significance—moral, spiritual, and aesthetic. He says it is given to "incite and to support the eternal", that it "is conscious of an indestructible dominion". In Book XIV of *The Prelude* he relates an experience on Snowdon, and upon this experience he models an account of the imagination. One summer night on the mountainside he saw the moon high up in the naked night sky looking down upon a sea of mist, through which the hills "their dusky backs upheaved": the vapours stretched over to the Atlantic which seemed to "give up his majesty". The moon, however, reigned supreme in the clear heaven. Through a rift in the vapours came the "roar of waters, torrents, streams" sounding in unison like one voice crying from the depths. Into this scene he read emblematic meanings. The moon resembled the human mind feeding "upon infinity" and hearing, as he had himself heard in his mystic states, nature speak, a

mind conscious of its power to penetrate matter—"In sense conducting
to ideal form"; but he read into the scene one function of the mind in
particular. Just as it seemed to him that the Atlantic submitted to the
authority of the vapours "stretched . . . in promontory shapes", so it
seemed that the vapours in their turn peacefully accepted the moon's
domination. This scene of "mutual domination" and "interchangeable supremacy" he defined as "power",

> . . . the express
> Resemblance of that glorious faculty
> That higher minds bear with them as their own.
> (*Prelude*, XIV, 88–90)

The faculty is imagination, and he goes on to explain how those with
"higher minds" use it: to transform, as the moon transforms the mist-
covered hills, to create a state or condition for themselves resembling
the moonlit scene, or, if such a scene presents itself to them without
their assistance, to recognize its glory and subject themselves to its
"inevitable mastery". Such minds (and he is thinking of poets specifically) use imagination to "build up greatest things From least suggestions", to be stirred but not enthralled by "sensible impressions" so
that the "spiritual world" opens before them. Such minds, filled with
the sense of their own creative power, possess a knowledge of the
spiritual life which enables them to formulate "moral judgments"
upon which rests a peace as profound as that brooding over the moonlit scene on Snowdon.

In all this Wordsworth speaks of himself as well as of "higher
minds". Ostensibly he is presenting, in blank verse, an analysis of the
workings of the imagination. By characterizing these workings as
creative, responsive, perceptive, selective, and plastic (in the sense of
holding, in mutual interchange, a number of different factors) he is, in
fact, describing his own mind. The moral certainties arose, for him,
from his perception of the cosmic force, a perception involving his
senses and his mind in a creative act. The act itself he now thinks of as
flowing from imagination, a word he uses as a convenient portmanteau
word. He packs into it deductions, which he elevates to the status of
general truths, from his own highly subjective and personal experience.

This is the way of the poet whose stock-in-trade is assertion. Words-worth's assertions, arising as they do from first-hand experience powerfully related, carry their own conviction. He is most matter-of-fact, and yet most concerned with the imponderables of our earthly existence. His words ring hard and clear, but with an echo of the beyond. Nowhere is this more in evidence than in *The Prelude*.

The Prelude

BEGUN in the winter of 1798–9 and completed in May 1805, *The Prelude* was not published until 1850, after the poet's death in April of that year. Between 1805 and 1850 Wordsworth returned again and again to the poem, revising and retouching it, until the text of 1850 contained many changes from that of 1805. These changes are important because they throw light on the development of his craft as a poet: they also indicate a retreat from political, religious, and philosophical positions held in 1805.

There are, therefore, two versions of *The Prelude*, the early one of 1805 and the final version of 1850. Published and edited together in one volume by Professor Ernest de Selincourt they provide, when compared, a sad commentary on the decline in Wordsworth's poetic powers, despite the fact that, as far as style is concerned, the 1850 text is generally an improvement on that of 1805. In his introduction, revised by Miss Helen Darbishire for the 1959 edition of *The Prelude*, Ernest de Selincourt summarizes these improvements as a strengthening of weak phrases, a tighter knitting of texture, and a clearer definition of thought. Against this he sets numerous examples of the very faults Wordsworth attacked in his Preface to the *Lyrical Ballads*, abstract language, unnatural diction, and elaborate periphrasis. One instance will serve to illustrate the extent of decline. The 1805 text contains this preface to the poet's encounter with the discharged soldier:

A favourite pleasure hath it been with me,
From time of earliest youth, to walk alone
Along the public Way, when, for the night

> Deserted, in its silence it assumes
> A character of deeper quietness
> Than pathless solitudes.

This, suggests Professor Selincourt, is "more in key with the bare impressive narrative" that is to follow than is the grandiloquent exordium of the later version. This exordium runs:

> When from our better selves we have too long
> Been parted by the hurrying world, and droop,
> Sick of its business, of its pleasures tired,
> How precious, how benign, is Solitude;

The retreat from political, religious, and philosophical positions comes out sharply in a comparison of the two versions. The young poet's faith in the ideals of the French Revolution are toned down. The brief account in the 1805 text of his return home to England is written up, in the later version, into a patriotic tribute to his native land. He adds a eulogy of Burke, the great opponent of the French Revolution.

In philosophical and religious matters the change is even more striking. As we have seen, the poet's mystic experience brought him into direct communion with a cosmic energy. Now at no time can this experience be properly described as Pantheism. Pantheism is a system, not a personal experience, a system in which the universe is conceived of as a whole made up of integrated parts. Pantheists deny the existence of a transcendent deity beyond the whole, although they may regard the whole as being itself divine or as containing a divine principle. A salient feature of the system is that, whatever element of divine is attributed to the whole, nothing resembling a personal God is admitted. Wordsworth's experience of cosmic energy was certainly an experience of wholeness, but it also seemed to him to be experience of a transcendent reality. What is more, he tended to personalize the reality as a Presence. The fact that he writes, poetically, in pantheistic terms, is merely his way of conveying a sense of the proximity of cosmic energy.

The philosophical system of Sensationalism, which supposes that sense-impressions produce spiritual and intellectual development and which is based upon a belief in the inherent goodness of human nature, is the nearest to Wordsworth's position. However, he did not embrace this system as such, though he was certainly influenced by it, and transformed some of its ideas, as put forward by its main exponent, David Hartley, into a personal philosophy of his own. As the intuition upon which this personal philosophy was founded began to fade, Wordsworth turned to the Christian faith. He had never opposed Christianity even though he had disliked crude orthodoxy: he simply did not bring it into his reckoning during his great years. But we can see from the last sections of the "Immortality Ode" (those written in 1805) and particularly from the "Ode to Duty" written in the same year, that a movement towards a more orthodox position is imminent. In this connection it is significant that he asks, in the Ode, for controls over his free-ranging spirit by way of rules of conduct.

The progress of his adoption of Christianity is clearly indicated by the changes in the 1850 version of *The Prelude*. The exuberant, positive faith of the independent thinker of 1798–1805 produced, in the 1805 version, unqualified references to "man's unconquerable mind", to "dignity", and "majesty", as Professor de Selincourt points out. In the later text such words are qualified because they seem contrary to the Christian virtue of meekness. Various words and phrases from the literature of conventional orthodoxy are worked into the poem in order to give the earlier statements a colour of Christianity. Professor de Selincourt writes:

In this spirit he adds a reference to matins and vespers (I, 45), includes among possible themes for poetic treatment "Christian meekness hallowing faithful loves" (I, 185), changes the simple phrase "as were a joy to hear" into the more elaborate

To which the silver wands of saints in Heaven
Might point with rapturous joy. (X, 485–6)

He alters anything sounding like the un-Christian creed of pantheism. He tones down the exuberant joy of the mystical passages.

These regrettable developments appear ironical in the light of *The*

Prelude's early history. Encouraged by Coleridge he intended to write a great philosophical poem to be entitled *The Recluse*. On 6 March 1798, he wrote to a friend, James Tobin:

> I have written 1,300 lines of a poem in which I contrive to convey most of the knowledge of which I am possessed.

Some of this material found its way into the poem we know as *The Prelude*. As a preliminary to the great philosophical *The Recluse*, Wordsworth conceived the idea of an autobiographical poem in five books, addressed to Coleridge. By 1800 he had completed the first two books. Until February 1804 he appears to have made little progress. He then tackled the work with ardour and vigour and except for a pause after the death of his brother John, completed it in thirteen books by May 1805. The "poem to Coleridge", as he and Dorothy called it, had vastly outgrown its original design: yet Wordsworth continued to speak of his great philosophical poem *The Recluse, or Views on Nature, Man and Society*. Dissatisfied with *The Prelude*, he decided to have it published posthumously. He embarked upon what he considered the second part of *The Recluse*, *The Prelude* being the first part. This second part became *The Excursion*, published in 1814, a poem generally much inferior to *The Prelude*.

The great project died, therefore, in the mediocrity of *The Excursion*, and the preliminary "poem to Coleridge", the true masterpiece, remained to Wordsworth a source of dissatisfaction. He tinkered with it for years, sensing, perhaps, that here lay his real achievement. After his death, his wife Mary named it *The Prelude* (1850). Wordsworth's grand philosophical poem became no more than the years of tinkering with its preliminary, years in which his skill remained to mock the genius long since dead.

In *The Prelude* Wordsworth attempted something entirely new, a history in verse of his mental and spiritual growth. The poem contains passages of prolixity, even tedious prolixity, as if Wordsworth found blank verse adapting itself too easily to the form of the eighteenth-century prose sentence. Interesting comparisons can be made between the prose of, say, the Preface to the *Lyrical Ballads* or the political tract on the Convention of Cintra and reflective passages in

The Prelude. Generally speaking, however, the verse of *The Prelude* moves vigorously and variously, the pause occurring rarely before the seventh syllable in overflow lines and more frequently between the second and sixth, so that the lines can be dove-tailed into rhythmic units matching the narrative. A story is by its nature a series of events requiring the special skill of a teller who never loses sight of the main objective; who, even when digressing, can pull his reader along by the momentum of what he relates. As a narrative poet Wordsworth is supreme: he can dispose details of place, person, or incident easily and smoothly without disturbing the flow of his main story. His "Michael" is excellent in this kind, but *The Prelude* contains numerous examples to equal it. Even the introductory inversion of:

> Midway on long Winander's eastern shore,
> Within the crescent of a pleasant bay,
> A tavern stood . . .
>
> (*Prelude*, II, 138–40)

deceptively easy to write, pulls us compellingly into lines full of detail:

> . . . no homely-featured house,
> Primeval like its neighbouring cottages
> But 'twas a splendid place, the door beset
> With chaises, grooms, and liveries, and within
> Decanters, glasses, and the blood-red wine.
>
> (*Prelude*, II, 140–4)

lines which, far from losing the rhythmic pulse of the narrative, strengthen it by slowing it to the inevitable pace required for an inventory. Of the many evocative, descriptive, reflective, and lyric passages much could be said: the remarkable fact is that these kinds of poetry occur together without striking us as incongruous. And it is no mean achievement that the enormous amount of information about the poet's life and thought never overwhelms.

The Prelude, unlike *Paradise Lost*, requires no critical apparatus to sustain and guide the modern reader. It can, and should, be taken up as a story and read fairly quickly. The miracle of growth and development, the magic and mystery of shore, hill, valley, and lake, the sweet hopes and eager idealism of youth, the vigorous and penetrating reflections of a mind always powerful, rarely vague, will utterly captivate the responsive reader, but what, above all, compels is the flavour of an original spirit at work. In speaking of his "own heart", Wordsworth conveys the special quality that makes him what he is. He sought consciously to do this, fired by the feeling of uniqueness which all men possess in some degree:

> Points have we all of us within our souls
> Where all stand single; this I feel, and make
> Breathings for incommunicable powers;
> But is not each a memory to himself?
>
> (*Prelude*, III, 185–88)

"Tintern Abbey", the "Immortality Ode", and *The Prelude* are rich in the true Wordsworthian tone, a prophetic high seriousness conveyed in the clear light of vision, based upon a firm sense of the concrete, and radiant with a wise innocence.

SUGGESTIONS FOR FURTHER READING

FURTHER reading should include "An Evening Walk", "Descriptive Sketches", and "Peter Bell", all referred to in the Introduction. The *Lyrical Ballads*, as they were published in 1798, are to be found in the Clarendon Press, Oxford edition, edited by H. Littledale (1911). The most convenient complete works is the one-volume edition of Thomas Hutchinson, Oxford University Press. Wordsworth's personal classification of his poems need not be too confusing. Ernest de Selincourt follows this classification in his definitive edition of the complete works in his five-volume edition, partly in conjunction with Helen Darbishire, Clarendon Press, Oxford (1940–54). Ernest de Selincourt's two-text edition of *The Prelude*, revised by Helen Darbishire, Clarendon Press, Oxford (1959), is indispensable to a detailed study of the poem. No serious student should neglect three other works: *The Letters of William Wordsworth* selected by Philip Wayne, Oxford

University Press (World's Classics) (1954); *The Journals of Dorothy Wordsworth* (2 vols.) edited by Ernest de Selincourt, Macmillan (1941); Coleridge's *Biographia Literaria*, particularly Chapters 14, 17–20 inclusive, and 22. Other reading might include:

HELEN DARBISHIRE, *The Poet Wordsworth.* Clarendon Press (Oxford, 1950).

H. W. GARROD, *Wordsworth: Lectures and Essays.* Clarendon Press (Oxford, 2nd ed. 1927).

BASIL WILLEY, *The Eighteenth-Century Background.* Chatto and Windus (London, 1940).

F. R. LEAVIS, *Revaluation.* Chatto and Windus (London, 1936).

F. W. BATESON, *Wordsworth: A Re-interpretation.* Longmans (London, 1963).

HERBERT READ, *The True Voice of Feeling.* Faber and Faber (London, 1953).

JOHN F. DANBY, *Wordsworth's "Prelude"* (*Studies in English Literature*). E. Arnold (London, 1963).

D. G. JAMES, *Scepticism and Poetry.* Allen and Unwin (London, 1960).

MARY MOORMAN, *William Wordsworth: A Biography.* Oxford University Press (London, 2 vols, 1957, 1965).

BIOGRAPHICAL NOTE

WILLIAM WORDSWORTH (1770–1850)

WILLIAM WORDSWORTH was the second in a family of four boys and a girl. He was born at Cockermouth, Cumberland, on 7 April 1770, a year and nine months before his sister Dorothy, who was to become, with his wife, his dearest companion. The Wordsworths were substantial middle-class people: John, the father, an attorney and agent to Sir James Lowther; Anne Cookson, the mother, a daughter of a Penrith mercer. John Wordsworth had originally come from Yorkshire.

The idyllic intensity of the poet's life with his sister and wife had something to do with the fact that he had lost both parents quite early. His mother died in 1778, his father in 1783. After his mother's death he was sent to the grammar school at Hawkshead, where he lodged with Anne Tyson (her name echoing that of his mother most appropriately). She mothered him, as we can see from the warm-hearted references to her in *The Prelude*. In 1787 he went up to St. John's College, Cambridge.

The family situation at the time he entered Cambridge was difficult. John Wordsworth's five children came under the guardianship of their uncles, Richard Wordsworth and Christopher Crackanthorp. They inherited very modest sums from their father together with a claim for £4,000 against the Lowther family (later to be met in full). The guardians hoped that William would enter the Church. He graduated successfully enough, if without distinction, in 1791, and produced his two poems "An Evening Walk" (1789) and "Descriptive Sketches" (1791–2). A walking-tour through France and Switzerland with his college friend Robert Jones during the summer vacation of 1790 had provided him with material for "Descriptive Sketches", but he made no attempt either to enter the Church or to embark upon any other recognized profession. Instead, he persuaded his uncles that he should learn French as a first step towards proficiency in languages. Accordingly, he visited France from November 1791 to December 1792, spending his time mostly at Orleans and Blois. At this time he met

Michel de Beaupuy, then a Captain (later a General) in the Revolutionary Army. Beaupuy's enthusiastic idealism struck a responsive chord in the young poet. He subscribed whole-heartedly to the aims of the Revolution, seeing in them, as he supposed, the beginning of man's ultimately successful rebellion against unjust social systems. Paradoxically he fell in love with the daughter of a royalist family, Annette Vallon, who bore him a daughter, Caroline, on 15 December 1792.

A depleted purse and impatient guardians drew him home in December 1792. England's declaration of war on France in February 1793 profoundly shocked him. The years that followed this event were a time of great moral and intellectual strain for him. His poem "Guilt and Sorrow", written during these years (1793–6), expressed the depth of his protest against social wrong. Gradual disillusionment with the Revolution led him into Godwinism during 1795. His reaction against this philosophy of rationalism produced a long period of depression from which Dorothy and Coleridge helped him to recover.

He had joined Dorothy on a visit to the Lakes in 1794. They had been apart more or less continuously since their mother's death in 1778 when Dorothy was placed with her mother's cousin, Mrs. Threlkeld, in Halifax. From 1787–8 she lived with her maternal grandparents at Penrith and then, rather more happily, with an uncle at Forncett, Norfolk (1788–93). She and William had been fond of each other from childhood. In 1795 they pooled their resources and went to live at Racedown, Dorsetshire; the £900 left to William by his friend, Raisley Calvert, proved most useful. It enabled him to forget the question of a career. Their neighbour proved to be Coleridge and soon they were all living near one another, the Wordsworths at Alfoxden, Coleridge at Nether Stowey.

The friendship of these three is one of the marvels of literary history. Dorothy's sensitive, simple, and deeply affectionate nature seems to have acted as a leaven and as a stimulus in the relationship that developed between the two poets. Together they produced the *Lyrical Ballads* in 1798 (Coleridge contributed "The Ancient Mariner"). They formulated an entirely new attitude to poets and poetry, expressed in Wordsworth's Preface to the 1800 edition of *Lyrical Ballads* and variously in Coleridge's *Biographia Literaria*.

After spending six months in Germany (1798–9), where the first parts of *The Prelude* were composed, William and Dorothy settled at Dove Cottage, Townend, Grasmere, in December 1799. It is likely that Books I and II of *The Prelude* were completed by the end of that year. During 1800 their brother John, whose death at sea was to have a profound effect upon them both, stayed with them from January to September. Coleridge had settled at Greta Hall, Keswick, and the friendship with him continued unabated. In 1802, Wordsworth married Mary Hutchinson. His five children were born at regular intervals until 1810. Two died in 1812 and a third, his daughter Dora, of whom he was especially fond, in 1847; only two, John and William, survived.

The surge of Wordsworth's poetic activity from 1798 to 1808 is remarkable. Between 1798 and 1800 he produced, besides the *Lyrical Ballads* and the first two books of *The Prelude*, Book I of *The Recluse* (published posthumously in 1883), "The Brothers", "Michael", and other poems. During 1802 and 1803 he composed thirty-nine poems, together with much of Books I and II of *The Excursion* (published in 1814), as well as sonnets, a form in which he excelled, though it was new to him. Books III to XIV of *The Prelude* were composed between February 1804 and May 1805 and "The Waggoner" between December 1806 and February 1807. In 1807 he published his *Poems in Two Volumes*. This great production included the "Immortality Ode" and the "Ode to Duty" but the *Edinburgh Review* savagely attacked it; indeed Wordsworth had to endure continuous and heavy attacks from reviewers until 1820 or thereabouts. After that date his fame grew and flourished. In 1843 he became Poet Laureate, succeeding his much inferior contemporary Southey.

Wordsworth's creative life after 1814 is marked by a craftsmanship of high order but undistinguished by genius. His *Ecclesiastical Sonnets*, composed mostly in 1821, are a far cry from the great works of 1802–5. The *River Duddon* series of Sonnets (1816–20) contain some pleasing pieces and at least one of outstanding merit, "Afterthought". The *Evening Voluntaries*, composed in the 1830s, are less impressive.

The ageing bard of firm conservatism in politics and exhaustingly lengthy poetic mediocrity is a depressing image, but one not without some basis in fact. Wordsworth is best remembered in his great days. His daily life at Grasmere was almost unbelievably idyllic. He appears to have lived in a state as near to complete happiness as human being ever can, and this with three women, his wife Mary, his sister Dorothy, and his wife's sister Sara. Dorothy read poetry to him and he to her: she related simple tales of her encounters with nature or people, out of which he created splendid works. He walked, generally alone, across the eternal hills. Dorothy's *Grasmere Journal* is a marvellous picture of their daily life. Here is a typical entry:

> *December 24th, Christmas Eve.* William is now sitting by me, at ½ past 10 o'clock. I have been beside him ever since tea running the heel of a stocking, repeating some of his sonnets to him, listening to his own repeating, reading some of Milton's, and the *Allegro* and *Penseroso*. It is a quiet keen frost. Mary is in the parlour below attending to the baking of cakes. . . . Sara is in bed with the tooth-ache. . . . My beloved William is turning over the leaves of Charlotte Smith's sonnets. . . .

Even Wordsworth's estrangement from Coleridge in 1810 ended in a satisfactory reconcilement in 1812. Nevertheless, as his letters show, he suffered his personal agonies and depressions as most other men. Dorothy fell seriously ill in 1829 and although she lived until 1855 never recovered her earlier powers. His wife Mary died in 1859. They both lived to see him die on 23 April 1850, and interred in the little churchyard of Grasmere Church.

THE POETRY OF WORDSWORTH

MARGARET, OR THE RUINED COTTAGE

Supine the Wanderer lay,
His eyes as if in drowsiness half shut,
The shadows of the breezy elms above
Dappling his face. He had not heard the sound
Of my approaching steps, and in the shade   5
Unnoticed did I stand some minutes' space.
At length I hailed him, seeing that his hat
Was moist with water-drops, as if the brim
Had newly scooped a running stream. He rose,
And ere our lively greeting into peace   10
Had settled, "'Tis", said I, "a burning day:
My lips are parched with thirst, but you, it seems,
Have somewhere found relief." He, at the word,
Pointing towards a sweet-briar, bade me climb
The fence where that aspiring shrub looked out   15
Upon the public way. It was a plot
Of garden ground run wild, its matted weeds
Marked with the steps of those, whom, as they passed,
The gooseberry trees that shot in long lank slips,
Or currants, hanging from their leafless stems, 20
In scanty strings, had tempted to o'erleap
The broken wall. I looked around, and there,
Where two tall hedge-rows of thick alder boughs
Joined in a cold damp nook, espied a well
Shrouded with willow-flowers and plumy fern.   25
My thirst I slaked, and, from the cheerless spot
Withdrawing, straightway to the shade returned
Where sate the old Man on the cottage-bench;
And, while, beside him, with uncovered head,
I yet was standing, freely to respire,   30
And cool my temples in the fanning air,
Thus did he speak. "I see around me here

Things which you cannot see: we die, my Friend,
Nor we alone, but that which each man loved
And prized in his peculiar nook of earth   35
Dies with him, or is changed; and very soon
Even of the good is no memorial left.
—The Poets, in their elegies and songs
Lamenting the departed, call the groves,
They call upon the hills and streams to mourn,   40
And senseless rocks; nor idly; for they speak,
In these their invocations, with a voice
Obedient to the strong creative power
Of human passion. Sympathies there are
More tranquil, yet perhaps of kindred birth,   45
That steal upon the meditative mind,
And grow with thought. Beside yon spring I stood,
And eyed its waters till we seemed to feel
One sadness, they and I. For them a bond
Of brotherhood is broken: time has been   50
When, every day, the touch of human hand
Dislodged the natural sleep that binds them up
In mortal stillness; and they ministered
To human comfort. Stooping down to drink,
Upon the slimy foot-stone I espied   55
The useless fragment of a wooden bowl;
Green with the moss of years, and subject only
To the soft handling of the elements:
There let it lie—how foolish are such thoughts!
Forgive them;—never—never did my steps   60
Approach this door but she who dwelt within
A daughter's welcome gave me, and I loved her
As my own child. Oh, Sir! the good die first,
And they whose hearts are dry as summer dust
Burn to the socket. Many a passenger   65
Hath blessed poor Margaret for her gentle looks,
When she upheld the cool refreshment drawn
From that forsaken spring; and no one came

But he was welcome; no one went away
But that it seemed she loved him. She is dead,   70
The light extinguished of her lonely hut,
The hut itself abandoned to decay,
And she forgotten in the quiet grave.

  "I speak", continued he, "of One whose stock
Of virtues bloomed beneath this lowly roof.   75
She was a Woman of a steady mind,
Tender and deep in her excess of love;
Not speaking much, pleased rather with the joy
Of her own thoughts: by some especial care
Her temper had been framed, as if to make   80
A Being, who by adding love to peace
Might live on earth a life of happiness.
Her wedded Partner lacked not on his side
The humble worth that satisfied her heart:
Frugal, affectionate, sober, and withal   85
Keenly industrious. She with pride would tell
That he was often seated at his loom,
In summer, ere the mower was abroad
Among the dewy grass,—in early spring,
Ere the last star had vanished.—They who passed   90
At evening, from behind the garden fence
Might hear his busy spade, which he would ply,
After his daily work, until the light
Had failed, and every leaf and flower were lost
In the dark hedges. So their days were spent   95
In peace and comfort; and a pretty boy
Was their best hope, next to the God in heaven.

  "Not twenty years ago, but you I think
Can scarcely bear it now in mind, there came
Two blighting seasons, when the fields were left   100
With half a harvest. It pleased Heaven to add
A worse affliction in the plague of war:

This happy Land was stricken to the heart!
A Wanderer then among the cottages,
I, with my freight of winter raiment, saw   105
The hardships of that season: many rich
Sank down, as in a dream, among the poor;
And of the poor did many cease to be,
And their place knew them not. Meanwhile, abridged
Of daily comforts, gladly reconciled   110
To numerous self-denials, Margaret
Went struggling on through those calamitous years
With cheerful hope, until the second autumn,
When her life's Helpmate on a sick-bed lay,
Smitten with perilous fever. In disease   115
He lingered long; and, when his strength returned,
He found the little he had stored, to meet
The hour of accident or crippling age,
Was all consumed. A second infant now
Was added to the troubles of a time   120
Laden, for them and all of their degree,
With care and sorrow: shoals of artisans
From ill-requited labour turned adrift
Sought daily bread from public charity,
They, and their wives and children—happier far   125
Could they have lived as do the little birds
That peck along the hedge-rows, or the kite
That makes her dwelling on the mountain rocks!

"A sad reverse it was for him who long
Had filled with plenty, and possessed in peace,   130
This lonely Cottage. At the door he stood,
And whistled many a snatch of merry tunes
That had no mirth in them; or with his knife
Carved uncouth figures on the heads of sticks—
Then, not less idly, sought, through every nook   135
In house or garden, any casual work
Of use or ornament; and with a strange,

Amusing, yet uneasy, novelty,
He mingled, where he might, the various tasks
Of summer, autumn, winter, and of spring.   140
But this endured not; his good humour soon
Became a weight in which no pleasure was:
And poverty brought on a petted mood
And a sore temper; day by day he drooped,
And he would leave his work—and to the town   145
Would turn without an errand his slack steps;
Or wander here and there among the fields.
One while he would speak lightly of his babes,
And with a cruel tongue: at other times
He tossed them with a false unnatural joy: 150
And 'twas a rueful thing to see the looks
Of the poor innocent children. 'Every smile',
Said Margaret to me, here beneath these trees,
'Made my heart bleed'."
            At this the Wanderer paused;
And, looking up to those enormous elms,   155
He said, "'Tis now the hour of deepest noon,
At this still season of repose and peace,
This hour when all things which are not at rest
Are cheerful; while this multitude of flies
With tuneful hum is filling all the air;   160
Why should a tear be on an old Man's cheek?
Why should we thus, with an untoward mind,
And in the weakness of humanity,
From natural wisdom turn our hearts away;
To natural comfort shut our eyes and ears;   165
And, feeding on disquiet, thus disturb
The calm of nature with our restless thoughts?"

   He spake with somewhat of a solemn tone:
But, when he ended, there was in his face
Such easy cheerfulness, a look so mild,   170
That for a little time it stole away

All recollection; and that simple tale
Passed from my mind like a forgotten sound.
A while on trivial things we held discourse,
To me soon tasteless. In my own despite,   175
I thought of that poor Woman as of one
Whom I had known and loved. He had rehearsed
Her homely tale with such familiar power,
With such an active countenance, an eye
So busy, that the things of which he spake   180
Seemed present; and, attention now relaxed,
A heart-felt chillness crept along my veins.
I rose; and, having left the breezy shade,
Stood drinking comfort from the warmer sun,
That had not cheered me long—ere, looking round   185
Upon that tranquil Ruin, I returned,
And begged of the old Man that, for my sake,
He would resume his story.

                         He replied,
"It were a wantonness, and would demand
Severe reproof, if we were men whose hearts   190
Could hold vain dalliance with the misery
Even of the dead; contented thence to draw
A momentary pleasure, never marked
By reason, barren of all future good.
But we have known that there is often found   195
In mournful thoughts, and always might be found,
A power to virtue friendly; were't not so,
I am a dreamer among men, indeed
An idle dreamer! 'Tis a common tale,
An ordinary sorrow of man's life,   200
A tale of silent suffering, hardly clothed
In bodily form.—But without further bidding
I will proceed.

               While thus it fared with them,
To whom this cottage, till those hapless years,
Had been a blessèd home, it was my chance   205

To travel in a country far remote;
And when these lofty elms once more appeared
What pleasant expectations lured me on
O'er the flat Common!—With quick step I reached
The threshold, lifted with light hand the latch;   210
But, when I entered, Margaret looked at me
A little while; then turned her head away
Speechless,—and, sitting down upon a chair,
Wept bitterly. I wist not what to do,
Nor how to speak to her. Poor Wretch! at last   215
She rose from off her seat, and then,—O Sir!
I cannot *tell* how she pronounced my name:—
With fervent love, and with a face of grief
Unutterably helpless, and a look
That seemed to cling upon me, she enquired   220
If I had seen her husband. As she spake
A strange surprise and fear came to my heart,
Nor had I power to answer ere she told
That he had disappeared—not two months gone.
He left his house: two wretched days had past,   225
And on the third, as wistfully she raised
Her head from off her pillow, to look forth,
Like one in trouble, for returning light,
Within her chamber-casement she espied
A folded paper, lying as if placed   230
To meet her waking eyes. This tremblingly
She opened—found no writing, but beheld
Pieces of money carefully enclosed,
Silver and gold. 'I shuddered at the sight',
Said Margaret, 'for I knew it was his hand   235
That must have placed it there; and ere that day
Was ended, that long anxious day, I learned,
From one who by my husband had been sent
With the sad news, that he had joined a troop
Of soldiers, going to a distant land.   240
—He left me thus—he could not gather heart

To take a farewell of me; for he feared
That I should follow with my babes, and sink
Beneath the misery of that wandering life.'

"This tale did Margaret tell with many tears: 245
And, when she ended, I had little power
To give her comfort, and was glad to take
Such words of hope from her own mouth as served
To cheer us both. But long we had not talked
Ere we built up a pile of better thoughts,   250
And with a brighter eye she looked around
As if she had been shedding tears of joy.
We parted.—'Twas the time of early spring;
I left her busy with her garden tools;
And well remember, o'er that fence she looked,   255
And, while I paced along the foot-way path,
Called out, and sent a blessing after me,
With tender cheerfulness, and with a voice
That seemed the very sound of happy thoughts.

"I roved o'er many a hill and many a dale,   260
With my accustomed load; in heat and cold,
Through many a wood and many an open ground,
In sunshine and in shade, in wet and fair,
Drooping or blithe of heart, as might befall;
My best companions now the driving winds,   265
And now the 'trotting brooks' and whispering trees,
And now the music of my own sad steps,
With many a short-lived thought that passed between,
And disappeared.
                    I journeyed back this way,
When, in the warmth of midsummer, the wheat   270
Was yellow, and the soft and bladed grass,
Springing afresh, had o'er the hay-field spread
Its tender verdure. At the door arrived,
I found that she was absent. In the shade,

Where now we sit, I waited her return.   275
Her cottage, then a cheerful object, wore
Its customary look,—only, it seemed,
The honeysuckle, crowding round the porch,
Hung down in heavier tufts; and that bright weed,
The yellow stone-crop, suffered to take root   280
Along the window's edge, profusely grew
Blinding the lower panes. I turned aside,
And strolled into her garden. It appeared
To lag behind the season, and had lost
Its pride of neatness. Daisy-flowers and thrift   285
Had broken their trim border-lines, and straggled
O'er paths they used to deck: carnations, once
Prized for surpassing beauty, and no less
For the peculiar pains they had required,
Declined their languid heads, wanting support.   290
The cumbrous bind-weed, with its wreaths and bells,
Had twined about her two small rows of peas,
And dragged them to the earth.
                              Ere this an hour
Was wasted.—Back I turned my restless steps;
A stranger passed; and, guessing whom I sought,   295
He said that she was used to ramble far.—
The sun was sinking in the west; and now
I sate with sad impatience. From within
Her solitary infant cried aloud;
Then, like a blast that dies away self-stilled,   300
The voice was silent. From the bench I rose;
But neither could divert nor soothe my thoughts.
The spot, though fair, was very desolate—
The longer I remained, more desolate:
And, looking round me, now I first observed   305
The corner stones, on either side the porch,
With dull red stains discoloured, and stuck o'er
With tufts and hairs of wool, as if the sheep,
That fed upon the Common, thither came

Familiarly, and found a couching-place   310
Even at her threshold. Deeper shadows fell
From these tall elms; the cottage-clock struck eight;—
I turned, and saw her distant a few steps.
Her face was pale and thin—her figure, too,
Was changed. As she unlocked the door, she said,   315
'It grieves me you have waited here so long,
But, in good truth, I've wandered much of late;
And, sometimes—to my shame I speak—have need
Of my best prayers to bring me back again.'
While on the board she spread our evening meal,   320
She told me—interrupting not the work
Which gave employment to her listless hands—
That she had parted with her elder child;
To a kind master on a distant farm
Now happily apprenticed.—'I perceive   325
You look at me, and you have cause; today
I have been travelling far; and many days
About the fields I wander, knowing this
Only, that what I seek I cannot find;
And so I waste my time: for I am changed;   330
And to myself', said she, 'have done much wrong
And to this helpless infant. I have slept
Weeping, and weeping have I waked; my tears
Have flowed as if my body were not such
As others are; and I could never die.   335
But I am now in mind and in my heart
More easy; and I hope', said she, 'that God
Will give me patience to endure the things
Which I behold at home.'
                              It would have grieved
Your very soul to see her. Sir, I feel   340
The story linger in my heart; I fear
'Tis long and tedious; but my spirit clings
To that poor Woman,—so familiarly
Do I perceive her manner, and her look,

And presence; and so deeply do I feel   345
Her goodness, that, not seldom, in my walks
A momentary trance comes over me;
And to myself I seem to muse on One
By sorrow laid asleep; or borne away,
A human being destined to awake   350
To human life, or something very near
To human life, when he shall come again
For whom she suffered. Yes, it would have grieved
Your very soul to see her: evermore
Her eyelids drooped, her eyes downward were cast;   355
And, when she at her table gave me food,
She did not look at me. Her voice was low,
Her body was subdued. In every act
Pertaining to her house-affairs, appeared
The careless stillness of a thinking mind   360
Self-occupied; to which all outward things
Are like an idle matter. Still she sighed,
But yet no motion of the breast was seen,
No heaving of the heart. While by the fire
We sate together, sighs came on my ear,   365
I knew not how, and hardly whence they came.

    "Ere my departure, to her care I gave,
For her son's use, some tokens of regard,
Which with a look of welcome she received;
And I exhorted her to place her trust   370
In God's good love, and seek his help by prayer.
I took my staff, and, when I kissed her babe,
The tears stood in her eyes. I left her then
With the best hope and comfort I could give:
She thanked me for my wish; but for my hope   375
It seemed she did not thank me.
                            I returned,
And took my rounds along this road again
When on its sunny bank the primrose flower

Peeped forth, to give an earnest of the Spring.
I found her sad and drooping: she had learned   380
No tidings of her husband; if he lived,
She knew not that he lived; if he were dead,
She knew not he was dead. She seemed the same
In person and appearance; but her house
Bespake a sleepy hand of negligence;   385
The floor was neither dry nor neat, the hearth
Was comfortless, and her small lot of books,
Which, in the cottage-window, heretofore
Had been piled up against the corner panes
In seemly order, now, with straggling leaves   390
Lay scattered here and there, open or shut,
As they had chanced to fall. Her infant Babe
Had from its mother caught the trick of grief,
And sighed among its playthings. I withdrew,
And once again entering the garden saw,   395
More plainly still, that poverty and grief
Were now come nearer to her: weeds defaced
The hardened soil, and knots of withered grass;
No ridges there appeared of clear black mould,
No winter greenness; of her herbs and flowers,   400
It seemed the better part were gnawed away
Or trampled into earth; a chain of straw,
Which had been twined about the slender stem
Of a young apple-tree, lay at its root;
The bark was nibbled round by truant sheep.   405
—Margaret stood near, her infant in her arms,
And, noting that my eye was on the tree,
She said, 'I fear it will be dead and gone
Ere Robert come again'. When to the House
We had returned together, she enquired   410
If I had any hope,—but for her babe
And for her little orphan boy, she said,
She had no wish to live, that she must die
Of sorrow. Yet I saw the idle loom

Still in its place; his Sunday garments hung   415
Upon the self-same nail; his very staff
Stood undisturbed behind the door.
                              And when,
In bleak December, I retraced this way,
She told me that her little babe was dead,
And she was left alone. She now, released   420
From her maternal cares, had taken up
The employment common through these wilds, and gained,
By spinning hemp, a pittance for herself;
And for this end had hired a neighbour's boy
To give her needful help. That very time   425
Most willingly she put her work aside,
And walked with me along the miry road,
Heedless how far; and, in such piteous sort
That any heart had ached to hear her, begged
That, wheresoe'er I went, I still would ask   430
For him whom she had lost. We parted then—
Our final parting; for from that time forth
Did many seasons pass ere I returned
Into this tract again.
                        Nine tedious years;
From their first separation, nine long years,   435
She lingered in unquiet widowhood;
A Wife and Widow. Needs must it have been
A sore heart-wasting! I have heard, my Friend,
That in yon arbour oftentimes she sate
Alone, through half the vacant sabbath day;   440
And, if a dog passed by, she still would quit
The shade, and look abroad. On this old bench
For hours she sate; and evermore her eye
Was busy in the distance, shaping things
That made her heart beat quick. You see that path,   445
Now faint,—the grass has crept o'er its grey line;
There, to and fro, she paced through many a day
Of the warm summer, from a belt of hemp

That girt her waist, spinning the long-drawn thread
With backward steps. Yet ever as there passed   450
A man whose garments showed the soldier's red,
Or crippled mendicant in sailor's garb,
The little child who sate to turn the wheel
Ceased from his task; and she with faltering voice
Made many a fond enquiry; and when they,   455
Whose presence gave no comfort, were gone by,
Her heart was still more sad. And by yon gate,
That bars the traveller's road, she often stood,
And when a stranger horseman came, the latch
Would lift, and in his face look wistfully: 460
Most happy, if, from aught discovered there
Of tender feeling, she might dare repeat
The same sad question. Meanwhile her poor Hut
Sank to decay; for he was gone, whose hand,
At the first nipping of October frost,   465
Closed up each chink, and with fresh bands of straw
Chequered the green-grown thatch. And so she lived
Through the long winter, reckless and alone;
Until her house by frost, and thaw, and rain,
Was sapped; and while she slept, the nightly damps   470
Did chill her breast; and in the stormy day
Her tattered clothes were ruffled by the wind,
Even at the side of her own fire. Yet still
She loved this wretched spot, nor would for worlds
Have parted hence; and still that length of road,   475
And this rude bench, one torturing hope endeared,
Fast rooted at her heart: and here, my Friend—
In sickness she remained; and here she died;
Last human tenant of these ruined walls!"

    The old Man ceased; he saw that I was moved;   480
From that low bench, rising instinctively
I turned aside in weakness, nor had power
To thank him for the tale which he had told.

I stood, and leaning o'er the garden wall
Reviewed that Woman's sufferings; and it seemed   485
To comfort me while with a brother's love
I blessed her in the impotence of grief.
Then towards the cottage I returned; and traced
Fondly, though with an interest more mild,
That secret spirit of humanity   490
Which, 'mid the calm oblivious tendencies
Of nature, 'mid her plants, and weeds, and flowers,
And silent overgrowings, still survived.
The old Man, noting this, resumed, and said,
"My Friend! enough to sorrow you have given,   495
The purposes of wisdom ask no more:
Nor more would she have craved as due to One
Who, in her worst distress, had ofttimes felt
The unbounded might of prayer; and learned, with soul
Fixed on the Cross, that consolation springs,   500
From sources deeper far than deepest pain,
For the meek Sufferer. Why then should we read
The forms of things with an unworthy eye?
She sleeps in the calm earth, and peace is here.
I well remember that those very plumes,   505
Those weeds, and the high spear-grass on that wall,
By mist and silent rain-drops silvered o'er,
As once I passed, into my heart conveyed
So still an image of tranquillity,
So calm and still, and looked so beautiful   510
Amid the uneasy thoughts which filled my mind,
That what we feel of sorrow and despair
From ruin and from change, and all the grief
That passing shows of Being leave behind,
Appeared an idle dream, that could maintain,   515
Nowhere, dominion o'er the enlightened spirit
Whose meditative sympathies repose
Upon the breast of Faith. I turned away,
And walked along my road in happiness."

THE OLD CUMBERLAND BEGGAR

I saw an aged Beggar in my walk;
And he was seated, by the highway side,
On a low structure of rude masonry
Built at the foot of a huge hill, that they
Who lead their horses down the steep rough road   5
May thence remount at ease. The aged Man
Had placed his staff across the broad smooth stone
That overlays the pile; and, from a bag
All white with flour, the dole of village dames,
He drew his scraps and fragments, one by one;   10
And scanned them with a fixed and serious look
Of idle computation. In the sun,
Upon the second step of that small pile,
Surrounded by those wild unpeopled hills,
He sat, and ate his food in solitude: 15
And ever, scattered from his palsied hand,
That, still attempting to prevent the waste,
Was baffled still, the crumbs in little showers
Fell on the ground; and the small mountain birds,
Not venturing yet to peck their destined meal,   20
Approached within the length of half his staff.

Him from my childhood have I known; and then
He was so old, he seems not older now;
He travels on, a solitary Man,
So helpless in appearance, that for him   25
The sauntering Horseman throws not with a slack
And careless hand his alms upon the ground,
But stops,—that he may safely lodge the coin
Within the old Man's hat; nor quits him so,
But still, when he has given his horse the rein,   30
Watches the aged Beggar with a look

Sidelong, and half-reverted. She who tends
The toll-gate, when in summer at her door
She turns her wheel, if on the road she sees
The aged Beggar coming, quits her work,   35
And lifts the latch for him that he may pass.
The post-boy, when his rattling wheels o'ertake
The aged Beggar in the woody lane,
Shouts to him from behind; and, if thus warned
The old man does not change his course, the boy   40
Turns with less noisy wheels to the road-side,
And passes gently by, without a curse
Upon his lips or anger at his heart.

    He travels on, a solitary Man;
His age has no companion. On the ground   45
His eyes are turned, and, as he moves along,
They move along the ground; and, evermore,
Instead of common and habitual sight
Of fields with rural works, of hill and dale,
And the blue sky, one little span of earth   50
Is all his prospect. Thus, from day to day,
Bow-bent, his eyes for ever on the ground,
He plies his weary journey; seeing still,
And seldom knowing that he sees, some straw,
Some scattered leaf, or marks which, in one track, 55
The nails of cart or chariot-wheel have left
Impressed on the white road,—in the same line,
At distance still the same. Poor Traveller!
His staff trails with him; scarcely do his feet
Disturb the summer dust; he is so still   60
In look and motion, that the cottage curs,
Ere he has passed the door, will turn away,
Weary of barking at him. Boys and girls,
The vacant and the busy, maids and youths,
And urchins newly breeched—all pass him by: 65
Him even the slow-paced waggon leaves behind.

But deem not this Man useless.—Statesmen! ye
Who are so restless in your wisdom, ye
Who have a broom still ready in your hands
To rid the world of nuisances; ye proud,   70
Heart-swoln, while in your pride ye contemplate
Your talents, power, or wisdom, deem him not
A burthen of the earth! 'Tis Nature's law
That none, the meanest of created things,
Of forms created the most vile and brute,   75
The dullest or most noxious, should exist
Divorced from good—a spirit and pulse of good,
A life and soul, to every mode of being
Inseparably linked. Then be assured
That least of all can aught—that ever owned   80
The heaven-regarding eye and front sublime
Which man is born to—sink, howe'er depressed,
So low as to be scorned without a sin;
Without offence to God cast out of view;
Like the dry remnant of a garden-flower   85
Whose seeds are shed, or as an implement
Worn out and worthless. While from door to door,
This old Man creeps, the villagers in him
Behold a record which together binds
Past deeds and offices of charity,   90
Else unremembered, and so keeps alive
The kindly mood in hearts which lapse of years,
And that half-wisdom half-experience gives,
Make slow to feel, and by sure steps resign
To selfishness and cold oblivious cares.   95
Among the farms and solitary huts,
Hamlets and thinly-scattered villages,
Where'er the aged Beggar takes his rounds,
The mild necessity of use compels
To acts of love; and habit does the work   100
Of reason; yet prepares that after-joy
Which reason cherishes. And thus the soul,

By that sweet taste of pleasure unpursued,
Doth find herself insensibly disposed
To virtue and true goodness.
                  Some there are,   105
By their good works exalted, lofty minds,
And meditative, authors of delight
And happiness, which to the end of time
Will live, and spread, and kindle: even such minds
In childhood, from this solitary Being,   110
Or from like wanderer, haply have received
(A thing more precious far than all that books
Or the solicitudes of love can do!)
That first mild touch of sympathy and thought,
In which they found their kindred with a world   115
Where want and sorrow were. The easy man
Who sits at his own door,—and, like the pear
That overhangs his head from the green wall,
Feeds in the sunshine; the robust and young,
The prosperous and unthinking, they who live   120
Sheltered, and flourish in a little grove
Of their own kindred;—all behold in him
A silent monitor, which on their minds
Must needs impress a transitory thought
Of self-congratulation, to the heart   125
Of each recalling his peculiar boons,
His charters and exemptions; and, perchance,
Though he to no one give the fortitude
And circumspection needful to preserve
His present blessings, and to husband up   130
The respite of the season, he, at least,
And 'tis no vulgar service, makes them felt.

  Yet further,—Many, I believe, there are
Who live a life of virtuous decency,
Men who can hear the Decalogue and feel   135
No self-reproach; who of the moral law

Established in the land where they abide
Are strict observers; and not negligent
In acts of love to those with whom they dwell,
Their kindred, and the children of their blood.   140
Praise be to such, and to their slumbers peace!
- -But of the poor man ask, the abject poor;
Go, and demand of him, if there be here
In this cold abstinence from evil deeds,
And these inevitable charities,   145
Wherewith to satisfy the human soul?
No—man is dear to man; the poorest poor
Long for some moments in a weary life
When they can know and feel that they have been,
Themselves, the fathers and the dealers-out   150
Of some small blessings; have been kind to such
As needed kindness, for this single cause,
That we have all of us one human heart.
—Such pleasure is to one kind Being known,
My neighbour, when with punctual care, each week,   155
Duly as Friday comes, though pressed herself
By her own wants, she from her store of meal
Takes one unsparing handful for the scrip
Of this old Mendicant, and, from her door
Returning with exhilarated heart,   160
Sits by her fire, and builds her hope in heaven.

   Then let him pass, a blessing on his head!
And while in that vast solitude to which
The tide of things has borne him, he appears
To breathe and live but for himself alone,   165
Unblamed, uninjured, let him bear about
The good which the benignant law of Heaven
Has hung around him: and, while life is his,
Still let him prompt the unlettered villagers
To tender offices and pensive thoughts.   170
—Then let him pass, a blessing on his head!

And, long as he can wander, let him breathe
The freshness of the valleys; let his blood
Struggle with frosty air and winter snows;
And let the chartered wind that sweeps the heath   175
Beat his grey locks against his withered face.
Reverence the hope whose vital anxiousness
Gives the last human interest to his heart.
May never HOUSE, misnamed of INDUSTRY,
Make him a captive!—for that pent-up din,   180
Those life-consuming sounds that clog the air,
Be his the natural silence of old age!
Let him be free of mountain solitudes;
And have around him, whether heard or not,
The pleasant melody of woodland birds.   185
Few are his pleasures: if his eyes have now
Been doomed so long to settle upon earth
That not without some effort they behold
The countenance of the horizontal sun,
Rising or setting, let the light at least   190
Find a free entrance to their languid orbs,
And let him, *where* and *when* he will, sit down
Beneath the trees, or on a grassy bank
Of highway side, and with the little birds
Share his chance-gathered meal; and, finally,   195
As in the eye of Nature he has lived,
So in the eye of Nature let him die!

SIMON LEE

THE OLD HUNTSMAN

In the sweet shire of Cardigan,
Not far from pleasant Ivor-hall,
An old Man dwells, a little man,—
'Tis said he once was tall.
Full five-and-thirty years he lived   5
A running huntsman merry;
And still the centre of his cheek
Is red as a ripe cherry.

No man like him the horn could sound,
And hill and valley rang with glee   10
When Echo bandied, round and round,
The halloo of Simon Lee.
In those proud days, he little cared
For husbandry or tillage;
To blither tasks did Simon rouse   15
The sleepers of the village.

He all the country could outrun,
Could leave both man and horse behind;
And often, ere the chase was done,
He reeled, and was stone-blind.   20
And still there's something in the world
At which his heart rejoices;
For when the chiming hounds are out,
He dearly loves their voices!

But, oh the heavy change!—bereft   25
Of health, strength, friends, and kindred, see!
Old Simon to the world is left
In liveried poverty.
His Master's dead,—and no one now
Dwells in the Hall of Ivor;   30
Men, dogs, and horses, all are dead;
He is the sole survivor.

And he is lean and he is sick;
His body, dwindled and awry,
Rests upon ankles swoln and thick;   35
His legs are thin and dry.
One prop he has, and only one,
His wife, an aged woman,
Lives with him, near the waterfall,
Upon the village Common.   40

Beside their moss-grown hut of clay,
Not twenty paces from the door,
A scrap of land they have, but they
Are poorest of the poor.
This scrap of land he from the heath   45
Enclosed when he was stronger;
But what to them avails the land
Which he can till no longer?

Oft, working by her Husband's side,
Ruth does what Simon cannot do;   50
For she, with scanty cause for pride,
Is stouter of the two.
And, though you with your utmost skill
From labour could not wean them,
'Tis little, very little—all   55
That they can do between them.

Few months of life has he in store
As he to you will tell,
For still, the more he works, the more
Do his weak ankles swell.   60
My gentle Reader, I perceive
How patiently you've waited,
And now I fear that you expect
Some tale will be related.

O Reader! had you in your mind   65
Such stores as silent thought can bring,
O gentle Reader! you would find
A tale in every thing.
What more I have to say is short,
And you must kindly take it: 70
It is no tale; but, should you think,
Perhaps a tale you'll make it.

One summer-day I chanced to see
This old Man doing all he could
To unearth the root of an old tree,   75
A stump of rotten wood.
The mattock tottered in his hand;
So vain was his endeavour,
That at the root of the old tree
He might have worked for ever.   80

"You're overtasked, good Simon Lee,
Give me your tool", to him I said;
And at the word right gladly he
Received my proffered aid.
I struck, and with a single blow   85
The tangled root I severed,
At which the poor old Man so long
And vainly had endeavoured.

The tears into his eyes were brought,
And thanks and praises seemed to run   90
So fast out of his heart, I thought
They never would have done.
—I've heard of hearts unkind, kind deeds
With coldness still returning;
Alas! the gratitude of men   95
Hath oftener left me mourning.

THE IDIOT BOY

'Tis eight o'clock,—a clear March night,
The moon is up,—the sky is blue,
The owlet, in the moonlight air,
Shouts from nobody knows where;
He lengthens out his lonely shout,   5
Halloo! halloo! a long halloo!

—Why bustle thus about your door,
What means this bustle, Betty Foy?
Why are you in this mighty fret?
And why on horseback have you set   10
Him whom you love, your Idiot Boy?

Scarcely a soul is out of bed;
Good Betty, put him down again;
His lips with joy they burr at you;
But, Betty! what has he to do   15
With stirrup, saddle, or with rein?

But Betty's bent on her intent;
For her good neighbour Susan Gale,
Old Susan, she who dwells alone,
Is sick, and makes a piteous moan,   20
As if her very life would fail.

There's not a house within a mile,
No hand to help them in distress;
Old Susan lies a-bed in pain,
And sorely puzzled are the twain,   25
For what she ails they cannot guess.

And Betty's husband's at the wood,
Where by the week he doth abide,
A woodman in the distant vale;
There's none to help poor Susan Gale;   30
What must be done? what will betide?

And Betty from the lane has fetched
Her Pony, that is mild and good;
Whether he be in joy or pain,
Feeding at will along the lane,   35
Or bringing faggots from the wood.

And he is all in travelling trim—
And, by the moonlight, Betty Foy
Has on the well-girt saddle set
(The like was never heard of yet)   40
Him whom she loves, her Idiot Boy.

And he must post without delay
Across the bridge and through the dale,
And by the church, and o'er the down,
To bring a Doctor from the town,   45
Or she will die, old Susan Gale.

There is no need of boot or spur,
There is no need of whip or wand;
For Johnny has his holly-bough,
And with a *hurly-burly* now   50
He shakes the green bough in his hand.

And Betty o'er and o'er has told
The Boy, who is her best delight,
Both what to follow, what to shun,
What do, and what to leave undone,   55
How turn to left, and now to right.

And Betty's most especial charge,
Was, "Johnny! Johnny! mind that you
Come home again, nor stop at all,—
Come home again, whate'er befall,   60
My Johnny, do, I pray you, do."

To this did Johnny answer make,
Both with his head and with his hand,
And proudly shook the bridle too;
And then! his words were not a few,   65
Which Betty well could understand.

And now that Johnny is just going,
Though Betty's in a mighty flurry,
She gently pats the Pony's side,
On which her Idiot Boy must ride,   70
And seems no longer in a hurry.

But when the Pony moved his legs,
Oh! then for the poor Idiot Boy!
For joy he cannot hold the bridle,
For joy his head and heels are idle,   75
He's idle all for very joy.

And, while the Pony moves his legs,
In Johnny's left hand you may see
The green bough motionless and dead:
The Moon that shines above his head   80
Is not more still and mute than he.

His heart it was so full of glee
That, till full fifty yards were gone,
He quite forgot his holly whip,
And all his skill in horsemanship: 85
Oh! happy, happy, happy John.

And while the Mother, at the door,
Stands fixed, her face with joy o'erflows,
Proud of herself, and proud of him,
She sees him in his travelling trim,   90
How quietly her Johnny goes.

The silence of her Idiot Boy,
What hopes it sends to Betty's heart!
He's at the guide-post—he turns right;
She watches till he's out of sight,   95
And Betty will not then depart.

Burr, burr—now Johnny's lips they burr,
As loud as any mill, or near it;
Meek as a lamb the Pony moves,
And Johnny makes the noise he loves,   100
And Betty listens, glad to hear it.

Away she hies to Susan Gale:
Her Messenger's in merry tune;
The owlets hoot, the owlets curr,
And Johnny's lips they burr, burr, burr,   105
As on he goes beneath the moon.

His steed and he right well agree;
For of this Pony there's a rumour
That, should he lose his eyes and ears,
And should he live a thousand years,   110
He never will be out of humour.

But then he is a horse that thinks!
And, when he thinks, his pace is slack;
Now, though he knows poor Johnny well,
Yet, for his life, he cannot tell   115
What he has got upon his back.

So through the moonlight lanes they go,
And far into the moonlight dale,
And by the church, and o'er the down,
To bring a Doctor from the town,   120
To comfort poor old Susan Gale.

And Betty, now at Susan's side,
Is in the middle of her story,
What speedy help her Boy will bring,
With many a most diverting thing,   125
Of Johnny's wit, and Johnny's glory.

And Betty, still at Susan's side,
By this time is not quite so flurried:
Demure with porringer and plate
She sits, as if in Susan's fate   130
Her life and soul were buried.

But Betty, poor good woman! she,
You plainly in her face may read it,
Could lend out of that moment's store
Five years of happiness or more   135
To any that might need it.

But yet I guess that now and then
With Betty all was not so well;
And to the road she turns her ears,
And thence full many a sound she hears,   140
Which she to Susan will not tell.

Poor Susan moans, poor Susan groans;
"As sure as there's a moon in heaven",
Cries Betty, "he'll be back again;
They'll both be here—'tis almost ten—   145
Both will be here before eleven."

Poor Susan moans, poor Susan groans;
The clock gives warning for eleven;
'Tis on the stroke—"He must be near",
Quoth Betty, "and will soon be here,   150
As sure as there's a moon in heaven."

The clock is on the stroke of twelve,
And Johnny is not yet in sight:
—The Moon's in heaven, as Betty sees,
But Betty is not quite at ease;   155
And Susan has a dreadful night.

And Betty, half an hour ago,
On Johnny vile reflections cast:
"A little idle sauntering Thing!"
With other names, an endless string;   160
But now that time is gone and past.

And Betty's drooping at the heart,
That happy time all past and gone,
"How can it be he is so late?
The Doctor, he has made him wait;   165
Susan! they'll both be here anon."

And Susan's growing worse and worse,
And Betty's in a sad *quandary*;
And then there's nobody to say
If she must go, or she must stay!   170
—She's in a sad *quandary*.

The clock is on the stroke of one;
But neither Doctor nor his Guide
Appears along the moonlight road;
There's neither horse nor man abroad,   175
And Betty's still at Susan's side

And Susan now begins to fear
Of sad mischances not a few,
That Johnny may perhaps be drowned;
Or lost, perhaps, and never found;   180
Which they must both for ever rue.

She prefaced half a hint of this
With "God forbid it should be true!"
At the first word that Susan said
Cried Betty, rising from the bed,   185
"Susan, I'd gladly stay with you.

"I must be gone, I must away:
Consider, Johnny's but half-wise;
Susan, we must take care of him,
If he is hurt in life or limb"—   190
"Oh God forbid!" poor Susan cries.

"What can I do?" says Betty, going,
"What can I do to ease your pain?
Good Susan tell me, and I'll stay;
I fear you're in a dreadful way,   195
But I shall soon be back again."

"Nay, Betty, go! good Betty, go!
There's nothing that can ease my pain."
Then off she hies; but with a prayer,
That God poor Susan's life would spare,   200
Till she comes back again.

So, through the moonlight lane she goes,
And far into the moonlight dale;
And how she ran, and how she walked,
And all that to herself she talked,   205
Would surely be a tedious tale.

In high and low, above, below,
In great and small, in round and square,
In tree and tower was Johnny seen,
In bush and brake, in black and green;   210
'Twas Johnny, Johnny, everywhere.

And while she crossed the bridge, there came
A thought with which her heart is sore—
Johnny perhaps his horse forsook,
To hunt the moon within the brook,   215
And never will be heard of more.

Now is she high upon the down,
Alone amid a prospect wide;
There's neither Johnny nor his Horse
Among the fern or in the gorse;   220
There's neither Doctor nor his Guide.

"Oh saints! what is become of him?
Perhaps he's climbed into an oak,
Where he will stay till he is dead;
Or sadly he has been misled,   225
And joined the wandering gipsy-folk.

"Or him that wicked Pony's carried
To the dark cave, the goblin's hall;
Or in the castle he's pursuing
Among the ghosts his own undoing;   230
Or playing with the waterfall."

At poor old Susan then she railed,
While to the town she posts away;
"If Susan had not been so ill,
Alas! I should have had him still,   235
My Johnny, till my dying day."

Poor Betty, in this sad distemper,
The Doctor's self could hardly spare:
Unworthy things she talked, and wild;
Even he, of cattle the most mild,   240
The Pony had his share.

But now she's fairly in the town,
And to the Doctor's door she hies;
'Tis silence all on every side;
The town so long, the town so wide,   245
Is silent as the skies.

And now she's at the Doctor's door,
She lifts the knocker, rap, rap, rap;
The Doctor at the casement shows
His glimmering eyes that peep and doze!   250
And one hand rubs his old night-cap.

"Oh Doctor! Doctor! where's my Johnny?"
"I'm here, what is't you want with me?"
"Oh Sir! you know I'm Betty Foy,
And I have lost my poor dear Boy,   255
You know him—him you often see;

D

He's not so wise as some folks be":
"The devil take his wisdom!" said
The Doctor, looking somewhat grim,
"What, Woman! should I know of him?"   260
And, grumbling, he went back to bed!

"O woe is me! O woe is me!
Here will I die; here will I die;
I thought to find my lost one here,
But he is neither far nor near,   265
Oh! what a wretched Mother I!"

She stops, she stands, she looks about;
Which way to turn she cannot tell.
Poor Betty! it would ease her pain
If she had heart to knock again;   270
—The clock strikes three—a dismal knell!

Then up along the town she hies,
No wonder if her senses fail;
This piteous news so much it shocked her,
She quite forgot to send the Doctor,   275
To comfort poor old Susan Gale.

And now she's high upon the down,
And she can see a mile of road:
"O cruel! I'm almost threescore;
Such night as this was ne'er before,   280
There's not a single soul abroad."

She listens, but she cannot hear
The foot of horse, the voice of man;
The streams with softest sound are flowing,
The grass you almost hear it growing,   285
You hear it now, if e'er you can.

The owlets through the long blue night
Are shouting to each other still:
Fond lovers! yet not quite hob nob,
They lengthen out the tremulous sob, 290
That echoes far from hill to hill.

Poor Betty now has lost all hope,
Her thoughts are bent on deadly sin,
A green-grown pond she just has past,
And from the brink she hurries fast, 295
Lest she should drown herself therein.

And now she sits her down and weeps;
Such tears she never shed before;
"Oh dear, dear Pony! my sweet joy!
Oh carry back my Idiot Boy! 300
And we will ne'er o'erload thee more."

A thought is come into her head:
The Pony he is mild and good,
And we have always used him well;
Perhaps he's gone along the dell, 305
And carried Johnny to the wood.

Then up she springs as if on wings;
She thinks no more of deadly sin;
If Betty fifty ponds should see,
The last of all her thoughts would be 310
To drown herself therein.

Oh Reader! now that I might tell
What Johnny and his Horse are doing!
What they've been doing all this time,
Oh could I put it into rhyme, 315
A most delightful tale pursuing!

THE POETRY OF WORDSWORTH

Perhaps, and no unlikely thought!
He with his Pony now doth roam
The cliffs and peaks so high that are,
To lay his hands upon a star,   320
And in his pocket bring it home.

Perhaps he's turned himself about,
His face unto his horse's tail,
And, still and mute, in wonder lost,
All silent as a horseman-ghost,   325
He travels slowly down the vale.

And now, perhaps, is hunting sheep,
A fierce and dreadful hunter he;
Yon valley, now so trim and green,
In five months' time, should be he seen,   330
A desert wilderness will be!

Perhaps, with head and heels on fire,
And like the very soul of evil,
He's galloping away, away,
And so will gallop on for aye,   335
The bane of all that dread the devil!

I to the Muses have been bound
These fourteen years, by strong indentures:
O gentle Muses! let me tell
But half of what to him befell;   340
He surely met with strange adventures.

O gentle Muses! is this kind?
Why will ye thus my suit repel?
Why of your further aid bereave me?
And can ye thus unfriended leave me;   345
Ye Muses! whom I love so well?

Who's yon, that, near the waterfall,
Which thunders down with headlong force,
Beneath the moon, yet shining fair,
As careless as if nothing were,   350
Sits upright on a feeding horse?

Unto his horse—there feeding free,
He seems, I think, the rein to give;
Of moon or stars he takes no heed;
Of such we in romances read: 355
—'Tis Johnny! Johnny! as I live.

And that's the very Pony, too!
Where is she, where is Betty Foy?
She hardly can sustain her fears;
The roaring waterfall she hears,   360
And cannot find her Idiot Boy.

Your Pony's worth his weight in gold:
Then calm your terrors, Betty Foy!
She's coming from among the trees,
And now all full in view she sees   365
Him whom she loves, her Idiot Boy.

And Betty sees the Pony too:
Why stand you thus, good Betty Foy?
It is no goblin, 'tis no ghost,
'Tis he whom you so long have lost,   370
He whom you love, your Idiot Boy.

She looks again—her arms are up—
She screams—she cannot move for joy;
She darts, as with a torrent's force,
She almost has o'erturned the Horse,   375
And fast she holds her Idiot Boy.

And Johnny burrs, and laughs aloud;
Whether in cunning or in joy
I cannot tell; but, while he laughs,
Betty a drunken pleasure quaffs   380
To hear again her Idiot Boy.

And now she's at the Pony's tail,
And now is at the Pony's head,—
On that side now, and now on this;
And, almost stifled with her bliss,   385
A few sad tears does Betty shed.

She kisses o'er and o'er again
Him whom she loves, her Idiot Boy;
She's happy here, is happy there,
She is uneasy everywhere;   390
Her limbs are all alive with joy.

She pats the Pony, where or when
She knows not, happy Betty Foy!
The little Pony glad may be,
But he is milder far than she,   395
You hardly can perceive his joy.

"Oh! Johnny, never mind the Doctor;
You've done your best, and that is all":
She took the reins, when this was said,
And gently turned the Pony's head   400
From the loud waterfall.

By this the stars were almost gone,
The moon was setting on the hill,
So pale you scarcely looked at her:
The little birds began to stir,   405
Though yet their tongues were still.

The Pony, Betty, and her Boy,
Wind slowly through the woody dale;
And who is she, betimes abroad,
That hobbles up the steep rough road?   410
Who is it, but old Susan Gale?

Long time lay Susan lost in thought;
And many dreadful fears beset her,
Both for her Messenger and Nurse;
And, as her mind grew worse and worse,   415
Her body—it grew better.

She turned, she tossed herself in bed,
On all sides doubts and terrors met her;
Point after point did she discuss;
And, while her mind was fighting thus,   420
Her body still grew better.

"Alas! what is become of them?
These fears can never be endured;
I'll to the wood."—The word scarce said,
Did Susan rise up from her bed,   425
As if by magic cured.

Away she goes up hill and down,
And to the wood at length is come;
She spies her Friends, she shouts a greeting;
Oh me! it is a merry meeting   430
As ever was in Christendom.

The owls have hardly sung their last,
While our four travellers homeward wend;
The owls have hooted all night long,
And with the owls began my song,   435
And with the owls must end.

For, while they all were travelling home,
Cried Betty, "Tell us, Johnny, do,
Where all this long night you have been,
What you have heard, what you have seen: 440
And, Johnny, mind you tell us true."

Now Johnny all night long had heard
The owls in tuneful concert strive;
No doubt too he the moon had seen;
For in the moonlight he had been   445
From eight o'clock till five.

And thus, to Betty's question, he
Made answer, like a traveller bold,
(His very words I give to you,)
"The cocks did crow to-whoo, to-whoo,   450
And the sun did shine so cold!"
—Thus answered Johnny in his glory,
And that was all his travel's story.

LINES

COMPOSED A FEW MILES ABOVE TINTERN ABBEY, ON REVISITING
THE BANKS OF THE WYE DURING A TOUR. JULY 13, 1798

Five years have past; five summers, with the length
Of five long winters! and again I hear
These waters, rolling from their mountain-springs
With a soft inland murmur.—Once again
Do I behold these steep and lofty cliffs,   5
That on a wild secluded scene impress

Thoughts of more deep seclusion; and connect
The landscape with the quiet of the sky.
The day is come when I again repose
Here, under this dark sycamore, and view   10
These plots of cottage-ground, these orchard-tufts,
Which at this season, with their unripe fruits,
Are clad in one green hue, and lose themselves
'Mid groves and copses. Once again I see
These hedge-rows, hardly hedge-rows, little lines   15
Of sportive wood run wild: these pastoral farms,
Green to the very door; and wreaths of smoke
Sent up, in silence, from among the trees!
With some uncertain notice, as might seem
Of vagrant dwellers in the houseless woods,   20
Or of some Hermit's cave, where by his fire
The Hermit sits alone.
                          These beauteous forms,
Through a long absence, have not been to me
As is a landscape to a blind man's eye:
But oft, in lonely rooms, and 'mid the din   25
Of towns and cities, I have owed to them,
In hours of weariness, sensations sweet,
Felt in the blood, and felt along the heart;
And passing even into my purer mind,
With tranquil restoration,—feelings too   30
Of unremembered pleasure: such, perhaps,
As have no slight or trivial influence
On that best portion of a good man's life,
His little, nameless, unremembered, acts
Of kindness and of love. Nor less, I trust,   35
To them I may have owed another gift,
Of aspect more sublime; that blessed mood,
In which the burthen of the mystery,
In which the heavy and the weary weight
Of all this unintelligible world,   40
Is lightened,—that serene and blessed mood,

In which the affections gently lead us on,—
Until, the breath of this corporeal frame
And even the motion of our human blood
Almost suspended, we are laid asleep   45
In body, and become a living soul:
While with an eye made quiet by the power
Of harmony, and the deep power of joy,
We see into the life of things.
                                If this
Be but a vain belief, yet, oh! how oft—   50
In darkness and amid the many shapes
Of joyless daylight; when the fretful stir
Unprofitable, and the fever of the world,
Have hung upon the beatings of my heart—
How oft, in spirit, have I turned to thee,   55
O sylvan Wye! thou wanderer thro' the woods,
How often has my spirit turned to thee!

    And now, with gleams of half-extinguished thought,
With many recognitions dim and faint,
And somewhat of a sad perplexity,   60
The picture of the mind revives again:
While here I stand, not only with the sense
Of present pleasure, but with pleasing thoughts
That in this moment there is life and food
For future years. And so I dare to hope,   65
Though changed, no doubt, from what I was when first
I came among these hills; when like a roe
I bounded o'er the mountains, by the sides
Of the deep rivers, and the lonely streams,
Wherever nature led: more like a man   70
Flying from something that he dreads than one
Who sought the thing he loved. For nature then
(The coarser pleasures of my boyish days,
And their glad animal movements all gone by)
To me was all in all,—I cannot paint   75

What then I was. The sounding cataract
Haunted me like a passion: the tall rock,
The mountain, and the deep and gloomy wood,
Their colours and their forms, were then to me
An appetite; a feeling and a love,   80
That had no need of a remoter charm,
By thought supplied, nor any interest
Unborrowed from the eye,—That time is past,
And all its aching joys are now no more,
And all its dizzy raptures. Not for this   85
Faint I, nor mourn nor murmur; other gifts
Have followed; for such loss, I would believe,
Abundant recompense. For I have learned
To look on nature, not as in the hour
Of thoughtless youth; but hearing often-times   90
The still, sad music of humanity,
Nor harsh nor grating, though of ample power
To chasten and subdue.   And I have felt
A presence that disturbs me with the joy
Of elevated thoughts; a sense sublime   95
Of something far more deeply interfused,
Whose dwelling is the light of setting suns,
And the round ocean and the living air,
And the blue sky, and in the mind of man:
A motion and a spirit, that impels   100
All thinking things, all objects of all thought,
And rolls through all things. Therefore am I still
A lover of the meadows and the woods,
And mountains; and of all that we behold
From this green earth; of all the mighty world   105
Of eye, and ear—both what they half create,
And what perceive; well pleased to recognize
In nature and the language of the sense
The anchor of my purest thoughts, the nurse,
The guide, the guardian of my heart, and soul   110
Of all my moral being.

                                                    Nor perchance,
If I were not thus taught, should I the more
Suffer my genial spirits to decay:
For thou art with me here upon the banks
Of this fair river; thou my dearest Friend,   115
My dear, dear Friend; and in thy voice I catch
The language of my former heart, and read
My former pleasures in the shooting lights
Of thy wild eyes. Oh! yet a little while
May I behold in thee what I was once,   120
My dear, dear Sister! and this prayer I make,
Knowing that Nature never did betray
The heart that loved her; 'tis her privilege,
Through all the years of this our life, to lead
From joy to joy: for she can so inform   125
The mind that is within us, so impress
With quietness and beauty, and so feed
With lofty thoughts, that neither evil tongues,
Rash judgments, nor the sneers of selfish men,
Nor greetings where no kindness is, nor all   130
The dreary intercourse of daily life,
Shall e'er prevail against us, or disturb
Our cheerful faith, that all which we behold
Is full of blessings. Therefore let the moon
Shine on thee in thy solitary walk;   135
And let the misty mountain-winds be free
To blow against thee: and, in after years,
When these wild ecstasies shall be matured
Into a sober pleasure; when thy mind
Shall be a mansion for all lovely forms,   140
Thy memory be as a dwelling-place
For all sweet sounds and harmonies; oh! then,
If solitude, or fear, or pain, or grief,
Should be thy portion, with what healing thoughts
Of tender joy wilt thou remember me,   145
And these my exhortations! Nor, perchance—

If I should be where I no more can hear
Thy voice, nor catch from thy wild eyes these gleams
Of past existence—wilt thou then forget
That on the banks of this delightful stream   150
We stood together; and that I, so long
A worshipper of Nature, hither came
Unwearied in that service: rather say
With warmer love—oh! with far deeper zeal
Of holier love. Nor wilt thou then forget   155
That after many wanderings, many years
Of absence, these steep woods and lofty cliffs,
And this green pastoral landscape, were to me
More dear, both for themselves and for thy sake!

THE LAST OF THE FLOCK

I

In distant countries have I been,
And yet I have not often seen
A healthy man, a man full grown,
Weep in the public roads, alone.
But such a one, on English ground,
And in the broad highway, I met;
Along the broad highway he came,
His cheeks with tears were wet:
Sturdy he seemed, though he was sad;
And in his arms a Lamb he had.

II

He saw me, and he turned aside,
As if he wished himself to hide:
And with his coat did then essay
To wipe those briny tears away.
I followed him, and said, "My friend,
What ails you? wherefore weep you so?"
—"Shame on me, Sir! this lusty Lamb,
He makes my tears to flow.
Today I fetched him from the rock;
He is the last of all my flock.

III

"When I was young, a single man,
And after youthful follies ran,
Though little given to care and thought,
Yet, so it was, an ewe I bought;
And other sheep from her I raised,
As healthy sheep as you might see;
And then I married, and was rich
As I could wish to be;
Of sheep I numbered a full score,
And every year increased my store.

IV

"Year after year my stock it grew;
And from this one, this single ewe,
Full fifty comely sheep I raised,
As fine a flock as ever grazed!
Upon the Quantock hills they fed;
They throve, and we at home did thrive:
—This lusty Lamb of all my store
Is all that is alive;
And now I care not if we die,
And perish all of poverty.

V

"Six Children, Sir! had I to feed;
Hard labour in a time of need!
My pride was tamed, and in our grief
I of the Parish asked relief.
They said, I was a wealthy man;
My sheep upon the uplands fed,
And it was fit that thence I took
Whereof to buy us bread.
'Do this: how can we give to you',
They cried, 'what to the poor is due?'

VI

"I sold a sheep, as they had said,
And bought my little children bread,
And they were healthy with their food;
For me—it never did me good.
A woeful time it was for me,
To see the end of all my gains,
The pretty flock which I had reared
With all my care and pains,
To see it melt like snow away—
For me it was a woeful day.

VII

"Another still! and still another!
A little lamb, and then its mother!
It was a vein that never stopped—
Like blood-drops from my heart they dropped.
Till thirty were not left alive
They dwindled, dwindled, one by one;
And I may say, that many a time
I wished they all were gone—
Reckless of what might come at last
Were but the bitter struggle past.

VIII

"To wicked deeds I was inclined,
And wicked fancies crossed my mind;
And every man I chanced to see,
I thought he knew some ill of me:
No peace, no comfort could I find,
No ease, within doors or without;
And crazily and wearily
I went my work about;
And oft was moved to flee from home,
And hide my head where wild beasts roam.

IX

"Sir! 'twas a precious flock to me,
As dear as my own children be;
For daily with my growing store
I loved my children more and more.
Alas! it was an evil time;
God cursed me in my sore distress;
I prayed, yet every day I thought
I loved my children less;
And every week, and every day,
My flock it seemed to melt away.

X

"They dwindled, Sir, sad sight to see!
From ten to five, from five to three,
A lamb, a wether, and a ewe;—
And then at last from three to two;
And, of my fifty, yesterday
I had but only one:
And here it lies upon my arm,
Alas! and I have none;—
To-day I fetched it from the rock;
It is the last of all my flock."

HER EYES ARE WILD

I

Her eyes are wild, her head is bare,
The sun has burnt her coal-black hair;
Her eyebrows have a rusty stain,
And she came far from over the main.
She has a baby on her arm,
Or else she were alone:
And underneath the hay-stack warm,
And on the greenwood stone,
She talked and sung the woods among,
And it was in the English tongue.

II

"Sweet babe! they say that I am mad,
But nay, my heart is far too glad,
And I am happy when I sing
Full many a sad and doleful thing:
Then, lovely baby, do not fear!
I pray thee have no fear of me;
But safe as in a cradle, here
My lovely baby! thou shalt be:
To thee I know too much I owe;
I cannot work thee any woe.

III

"A fire was once within my brain;
And in my head a dull, dull pain;
And fiendish faces, one, two, three,
Hung at my breast, and pulled at me;

But then there came a sight of joy;
It came at once to do me good;
I waked, and saw my little boy,
My little boy of flesh and blood;
Oh joy for me that sight to see!
For he was here, and only he.

IV

"Suck, little babe, oh suck again!
It cools my blood; it cools my brain;
Thy lips I feel them, baby! they
Draw from my heart the pain away.
Oh! press me with thy little hand;
It loosens something at my chest;
About that tight and deadly band
I feel thy little fingers prest.
The breeze I see is in the tree:
It comes to cool my babe and me.

V

"Oh! love me, love me, little boy!
Thou art thy mother's only joy;
And do not dread the waves below,
When o'er the sea-rock's edge we go;
The high crag cannot work me harm,
Nor leaping torrents when they howl;
The babe I carry on my arm,
He saves for me my precious soul;
Then happy lie; for blest am I;
Without me my sweet babe would die.

VI

"Then do not fear, my boy! for thee
Bold as a lion will I be;
And I will always be thy guide,
Through hollow snows and rivers wide.

I'll build an Indian bower; I know
The leaves that make the softest bed:
And if from me thou wilt not go,
But still be true till I am dead,
My pretty thing! then thou shalt sing
As merry as the birds in spring.

VII

"Thy father cares not for my breast,
'Tis thine, sweet baby, there to rest;
'Tis all thine own!—and if its hue
Be changed, that was so fair to view,
'Tis fair enough for thee, my dove!
My beauty, little child, is flown,
But thou wilt live with me in love;
And what if my poor cheek be brown?
'Tis well for me thou canst not see
How pale and wan it else would be.

VIII

"Dread not their taunts, my little Life;
I am thy father's wedded wife;
And underneath the spreading tree
We two will live in honesty.
If his sweet boy he could forsake,
With me he never would have stayed:
From him no harm my babe can take;
But he, poor man! is wretched made;
And every day we two will pray
For him that's gone and far away.

IX

"I'll teach my boy the sweetest things:
I'll teach him how the owlet sings.
My little babe! thy lips are still,
And thou hast almost sucked thy fill.

—Where art thou gone, my own dear child?
What wicked looks are those I see?
Alas! Alas! that look so wild,
It never, never came from me:
If thou art mad, my pretty lad,
Then I must be for ever sad.

X

"Oh! smile on me, my little lamb!
For I thy own dear mother am:
My love for thee has well been tried:
I've sought thy father far and wide.
I know the poisons of the shade;
I know the earth-nuts fit for food:
Then, pretty dear, be not afraid:
We'll find thy father in the wood.
Now laugh and be gay, to the woods away!
And there, my babe, we'll live for aye."

THE COMPLAINT

OF A FORSAKEN INDIAN WOMAN

I

Before I see another day,
Oh let my body die away!
In sleep I heard the northern gleams;
The stars, they were among my dreams;
In rustling conflict through the skies,
I heard, I saw the flashes drive,

And yet they are upon my eyes,
And yet I am alive;
Before I see another day,
Oh let my body die away!

II

My fire is dead: it knew no pain;
Yet is it dead, and I remain:
All stiff with ice the ashes lie;
And they are dead, and I will die.
When I was well, I wished to live,
For clothes, for warmth, for food, and fire;
But they to me no joy can give,
No pleasure now, and no desire.
Then here contented will I lie!
Alone, I cannot fear to die.

III

Alas! ye might have dragged me on
Another day, a single one!
Too soon I yielded to despair;
Why did ye listen to my prayer?
When ye were gone my limbs were stronger;
And oh, how grievously I rue,
That, afterwards, a little longer,
My friends, I did not follow you!
For strong and without pain I lay,
Dear friends, when ye were gone away.

IV

My Child! they gave thee to another,
A woman who was not thy mother.
When from my arms my Babe they took,
On me how strangely did he look!
Through his whole body something ran,
A most strange working did I see;

—As if he strove to be a man,
That he might pull the sledge for me:
And then he stretched his arms, how wild!
Oh mercy! like a helpless child.

V

My little joy! my little pride!
In two days more I must have died.
Then do not weep and grieve for me;
I feel I must have died with thee.
O wind, that o'er my head art flying
The way my friends their course did bend,
I should not feel the pain of dying,
Could I with thee a message send;
Too soon, my friends, ye went away;
For I had many things to say.

VI

I'll follow you across the snow;
Ye travel heavily and slow;
In spite of all my weary pain
I'll look upon your tents again.
—My fire is dead, and snowy white
The water which beside it stood:
The wolf has come to me tonight,
And he has stolen away my food.
For ever left alone am I;
Then wherefore should I fear to die?

VII

Young as I am, my course is run,
I shall not see another sun;
I cannot lift my limbs to know
If they have any life or no.
My poor forsaken Child, if I
For once could have thee close to me,

With happy heart I then would die,
And my last thought would happy be;
But thou, dear Babe, art far away,
Nor shall I see another day.

NUTTING

It seems a day
(I speak of one from many singled out)
One of those heavenly days that cannot die;
When, in the eagerness of boyish hope,
I left our cottage-threshold, sallying forth   5
With a huge wallet o'er my shoulders slung,
A nutting-crook in hand; and turned my steps
Tow'rd some far-distant wood, a Figure quaint,
Tricked out in proud disguise of cast-off weeds
Which for that service had been husbanded,   10
By exhortation of my frugal Dame—
Motley accoutrement, of power to smile
At thorns, and brakes, and brambles,—and in truth
More ragged than need was! O'er pathless rocks,
Through beds of matted fern, and tangled thickets,   15
Forcing my way, I came to one dear nook
Unvisited, where not a broken bough
Drooped with its withered leaves, ungracious sign
Of devastation; but the hazels rose
Tall and erect, with tempting clusters hung,   20
A virgin scene!—A little while I stood,
Breathing with such suppression of the heart
As joy delights in; and with wise restraint
Voluptuous, fearless of a rival, eyed
The banquet;—or beneath the trees I sate   25
Among the flowers, and with the flowers I played;

A temper known to those who, after long
And weary expectation, have been blest
With sudden happiness beyond all hope.
Perhaps it was a bower beneath whose leaves   30
The violets of five seasons re-appear
And fade, unseen by any human eye;
Where fairy water-breaks do murmur on
For ever; and I saw the sparkling foam,
And—with my cheek on one of those green stones   35
That, fleeced with moss, under the shady trees,
Lay round me, scattered like a flock of sheep—
I heard the murmur and the murmuring sound,
In that sweet mood when pleasure loves to pay
Tribute to ease: and, of its joy secure,   40
The heart luxuriates with indifferent things,
Wasting its kindliness on stocks and stones,
And on the vacant air. Then up I rose,
And dragged to earth both branch and bough, with crash
And merciless ravage: and the shady nook   45
Of hazels, and the green and mossy bower,
Deformed and sullied, patiently gave up
Their quiet being: and unless I now
Confound my present feelings with the past,
Ere from the mutilated bower I turned   50
Exulting, rich beyond the wealth of kings,
I felt a sense of pain when I beheld
The silent trees, and saw the intruding sky.—
Then, dearest Maiden, move along these shades
In gentleness of heart; with gentle hand   55
Touch—for there is a spirit in the woods.

THERE WAS A BOY

There was a Boy; ye knew him well, ye cliffs
And islands of Winander!—many a time,
At evening, when the earliest stars began
To move along the edges of the hills,
Rising or setting, would he stand alone,   5
Beneath the trees, or by the glimmering lake;
And there, with fingers interwoven, both hands
Pressed closely palm to palm and to his mouth
Uplifted, he, as through an instrument,
Blew mimic hootings to the silent owls,   10
That they might answer him.—And they would shout
Across the watery vale, and shout again,
Responsive to his call,—with quivering peals,
And long halloos, and screams, and echoes loud
Redoubled and redoubled; concourse wild   15
Of jocund din! And, when there came a pause
Of silence such as baffled his best skill:
Then sometimes, in that silence, while he hung
Listening, a gentle shock of mild surprise
Has carried far into his heart the voice   20
Of mountain-torrents; or the visible scene
Would enter unawares into his mind
With all its solemn imagery, its rocks,
Its woods, and that uncertain heaven received
Into the bosom of the steady lake.   25

   This boy was taken from his mates, and died
In childhood, ere he was full twelve years old.

Pre-eminent in beauty is the vale
Where he was born and bred: the churchyard hangs
Upon a slope above the village-school;   30
And through that churchyard when my way has led
On summer-evenings, I believe that there
A long half-hour together I have stood
Mute—looking at the grave in which he lies!

Lucy Poems

Strange fits of passion have I known:
And I will dare to tell,
But in the Lover's ear alone,
What once to me befell.

When she I loved looked every day
Fresh as a rose in June,
I to her cottage bent my way,
Beneath an evening-moon.

Upon the moon I fixed my eye,
All over the wide lea;
With quickening pace my horse drew nigh
Those paths so dear to me.

And now we reached the orchard-plot;
And, as we climbed the hill,
The sinking moon to Lucy's cot
Came near, and nearer still.

In one of those sweet dreams I slept,
Kind Nature's gentlest boon!
And all the while my eyes I kept
On the descending moon.

My horse moved on; hoof after hoof
He raised, and never stopped:
When down behind the cottage roof,
At once, the bright moon dropped.

What fond and wayward thoughts will slide
Into a Lover's head!
"O mercy!" to myself I cried,
"If Lucy should be dead!"

*

She dwelt among the untrodden ways
    Beside the springs of Dove,
A Maid whom there were none to praise
    And very few to love:

A violet by a mossy stone
    Half hidden from the eye!
—Fair as a star, when only one
    Is shining in the sky.

She lived unknown, and few could know
    When Lucy ceased to be;
But she is in her grave, and, oh,
    The difference to me!

*

I travelled among unknown men,
    In lands beyond the sea;
Nor, England! did I know till then
    What love I bore to thee.

'Tis past, that melancholy dream!
    Nor will I quit thy shore
A second time; for still I seem
    To love thee more and more.

Among thy mountains did I feel
    The joy of my desire;
And she I cherished turned her wheel
    Beside an English fire.

Thy mornings showed, thy nights concealed,
  The bowers where Lucy played;
And thine too is the last green field
  That Lucy's eyes surveyed.

                    *

Three years she grew in sun and shower,
Then Nature said, "A lovelier flower
On earth was never sown;
This Child I to myself will take;
She shall be mine, and I will make
A Lady of my own.

"Myself will to my darling be
Both law and impulse: and with me
The Girl, in rock and plain,
In earth and heaven, in glade and bower,
Shall feel an overseeing power
To kindle or restrain.

"She shall be sportive as the fawn
That wild with glee across the lawn
Or up the mountain springs;
And hers shall be the breathing balm,
And hers the silence and the calm
Of mute insensate things.

"The floating clouds their state shall lend
To her; for her the willow bend;
Nor shall she fail to see
Even in the motions of the Storm
Grace that shall mould the Maiden's form
By silent sympathy.

"The stars of midnight shall be dear
To her; and she shall lean her ear

In many a secret place
Where rivulets dance their wayward round,
And beauty born of murmuring sound
Shall pass into her face.

"And vital feelings of delight
Shall rear her form to stately height,
Her virgin bosom swell;
Such thoughts to Lucy I will give
While she and I together live
Here in this happy dell."

Thus Nature spake—The work was done—
How soon my Lucy's race was run!
She died, and left to me
This heath, this calm, and quiet scene;
The memory of what has been,
And never more will be.

*

A slumber did my spirit seal;
  I had no human fears:
She seemed a thing that could not feel
  The touch of earthly years.

No motion has she now, no force;
  She neither hears nor sees;
Rolled round in earth's diurnal course,
  With rocks, and stones, and trees.

RUTH

When Ruth was left half desolate,
Her Father took another Mate;
And Ruth, not seven years old,
A slighted child, at her own will
Went wandering over dale and hill,   5
In thoughtless freedom, bold.

And she had made a pipe of straw,
And music from that pipe could draw
Like sounds of winds and floods;
Had built a bower upon the green,   10
As if she from her birth had been
An infant of the woods.

Beneath her father's roof, alone
She seemed to live; her thoughts her own;
Herself her own delight;   15
Pleased with herself, nor sad, nor gay;
And, passing thus the live-long day,
She grew to woman's height.

There came a Youth from Georgia's shore—
A military casque he wore,   20
With splendid feathers drest;
He brought them from the Cherokees;
The feathers nodded in the breeze,
And made a gallant crest.

From Indian blood you deem him sprung: 25
But no! he spake the English tongue,
And bore a soldier's name;
And, when America was free
From battle and from jeopardy,
He 'cross the ocean came.   30

With hues of genius on his cheek
In finest tones the Youth could speak:
—While he was yet a boy,
The moon, the glory of the sun,
And streams that murmur as they run,   35
Had been his dearest joy.

He was a lovely Youth! I guess
The panther in the wilderness
Was not so fair as he;
And, when he chose to sport and play,   40
No dolphin ever was so gay
Upon the tropic sea.

Among the Indians he had fought,
And with him many tales he brought
Of pleasure and of fear;   45
Such tales as told to any maid
By such a Youth, in the green shade,
Were perilous to hear.

He told of girls—a happy rout!
Who quit their fold with dance and shout,   50
Their pleasant Indian town,
To gather strawberries all day long;
Returning with a choral song
When daylight is gone down.

He spake of plants that hourly change   55
Their blossoms, through a boundless range
Of intermingling hues;
With budding, fading, faded flowers
They stand the wonder of the bowers
From morn to evening dews.   60

He told of the magnolia, spread
High as a cloud, high over head!
The cypress and her spire;
—Of flowers that with one scarlet gleam
Cover a hundred leagues, and seem   65
To set the hills on fire.

The Youth of green savannahs spake,
And many an endless, endless lake,
With all its fairy crowds
Of islands, that together lie   70
As quietly as spots of sky
Among the evening clouds.

"How pleasant", then he said, "it were
A fisher or a hunter there,
In sunshine or in shade   75
To wander with an easy mind;
And build a household fire, and find
A home in every glade!

"What days and what bright years! Ah me!
Our life were life indeed, with thee   80
So passed in quiet bliss,
And all the while", said he, "to know
That we were in a world of woe,
On such an earth as this!"

E

And then he sometimes interwove   85
Fond thoughts about a father's love:
"For there", said he, "are spun
Around the heart such tender ties,
That our own children to our eyes
Are dearer than the sun.   90

"Sweet Ruth! and could you go with me
My helpmate in the woods to be,
Our shed at night to rear;
Or run, my own adopted bride,
A sylvan huntress at my side,   95
And drive the flying deer!

"Beloved Ruth!"—No more he said.
The wakeful Ruth at midnight shed
A solitary tear:
She thought again—and did agree   100
With him to sail across the sea,
And drive the flying deer.

"And now, as fitting is and right,
We in the church our faith will plight,
A husband and a wife."   105
Even so they did; and I may say
That to sweet Ruth that happy day
Was more than human life.

Through dream and vision did she sink,
Delighted all the while to think   110
That on those lonesome floods,
And green savannahs, she should share
His board with lawful joy, and bear
His name in the wild woods.

But, as you have before been told,   115
This Stripling, sportive, gay, and bold,
And, with his dancing crest,
So beautiful, through savage lands
Had roamed about, with vagrant bands
Of Indians in the West.   120

The wind, the tempest roaring high,
The tumult of a tropic sky,
Might well be dangerous food
For him, a Youth to whom was given
So much of earth—so much of heaven,   125
And such impetuous blood.

Whatever in those climes he found
Irregular in sight or sound
Did to his mind impart
A kindred impulse, seemed allied   130
To his own powers, and justified
The workings of his heart.

Nor less, to feed voluptuous thought.
The beauteous forms of nature wrought,
Fair trees and gorgeous flowers;   135
The breezes their own languor lent;
The stars had feelings, which they sent
Into those favoured bowers.

Yet, in his worst pursuits I ween
That sometimes there did intervene   140
Pure hopes of high intent:
For passions linked to forms so fair
And stately needs must have their share
Of noble sentiment.

But ill he lived, much evil saw,   145
With men to whom no better law
Nor better life was known;
Deliberately, and undeceived,
Those wild men's vices he received,
And gave them back his own.   150

His genius and his moral frame
Were thus impaired, and he became
The slave of low desires:
A Man who without self-control
Would seek what the degraded soul   155
Unworthily admires.

And yet he with no feigned delight
Had wooed the Maiden, day and night
Had loved her, night and morn:
What could he less than love a Maid   160
Whose heart with so much nature played?
So kind and so forlorn!

Sometimes, most earnestly, he said,
"O Ruth! I have been worse than dead;
False thoughts, thoughts bold and vain,   165
Encompassed me on every side
When I, in confidence and pride,
Had crossed the Atlantic main.

"Before me shone a glorious world—
Fresh as a banner bright, unfurled   170
To music suddenly:
I looked upon those hills and plains,
And seemed as if let loose from chains,
To live at liberty.

"No more of this; for now, by thee   175
Dear Ruth! more happily set free
With nobler zeal I burn;
My soul from darkness is released,
Like the whole sky when to the east
The morning doth return."   180

Full soon that better mind was gone:
No hope, no wish remained, not one—
They stirred him now no more;
New objects did new pleasure give,
And once again he wished to live   185
As lawless as before.

Meanwhile, as thus with him it fared,
They for the voyage were prepared,
And went to the sea-shore,
But, when they thither came, the Youth   190
Deserted his poor Bride, and Ruth
Could never find him more.

God help thee, Ruth!—Such pains she had,
That she in half a year was mad,
And in a prison housed;   195
And there, with many a doleful song
Made of wild words, her cup of wrong
She fearfully caroused.

Yet sometimes milder hours she knew,
Nor wanted sun, nor rain, nor dew,   200
Nor pastimes of the May;
—They all were with her in her cell;
And a clear brook with cheerful knell
Did o'er the pebbles play.

When Ruth three seasons thus had lain,   205
There came a respite to her pain;
She from her prison fled;
But of the Vagrant none took thought;
And where it liked her best she sought
Her shelter and her bread.   210

Among the fields she breathed again:
The master-current of her brain
Ran permanent and free;
And, coming to the Banks of Tone,
There did she rest; and dwell alone   215
Under the greenwood tree.

The engines of her pain, the tools
That shaped her sorrow, rocks and pools,
And airs that gently stir
The vernal leaves—she loved them still;   220
Nor ever taxed them with the ill
Which had been done to her.

A Barn her *winter* bed supplies;
But, till the warmth of summer skies
And summer days is gone,   225
(And all do in this tale agree)
She sleeps beneath the greenwood tree,
And other home hath none.

An innocent life, yet far astray!
And Ruth will, long before her day,   230
Be broken down and old:
Sore aches she needs must have! but less
Of mind than body's wretchedness,
From damp, and rain, and cold.

If she is prest by want of food,   235
She from her dwelling in the wood
Repairs to a road-side;
And there she begs at one steep place
Where up and down with easy pace
The horsemen-travellers ride.   240

That oaten pipe of hers is mute,
Or thrown away; but with a flute
Her loneliness she cheers:
This flute, made of a hemlock stalk,
At evening in his homeward walk   245
The Quantock woodman hears.

I, too, have passed her on the hills
Setting her little water-mills
By spouts and fountains wild—
Such small machinery as she turned   250
Ere she had wept, ere she had mourned,
A young and happy Child!

Farewell! and when thy days are told,
Ill-fated Ruth, in hallowed mould
Thy corpse shall buried be,   255
For thee a funeral bell shall ring,
And all the congregation sing
A Christian psalm for thee.

MICHAEL

A PASTORAL POEM

If from the public way you turn your steps
Up the tumultuous brook of Green-head Ghyll,
You will suppose that with an upright path
Your feet must struggle; in such bold ascent
The pastoral mountains front you, face to face.   5
But, courage! for around that boisterous brook
The mountains have all opened out themselves,
And made a hidden valley of their own.
No habitation can be seen; but they
Who journey thither find themselves alone   10
With a few sheep, with rocks and stones, and kites
That overhead are sailing in the sky.
It is in truth an utter solitude;
Nor should I have made mention of this Dell
But for one object which you might pass by,   15
Might see and notice not. Beside the brook
Appears a straggling heap of unhewn stones!
And to that simple object appertains
A story—unenriched with strange events,
Yet not unfit, I deem, for the fireside,   20
Or for the summer shade. It was the first
Of those domestic tales that spake to me
Of Shepherds, dwellers in the valleys, men
Whom I already loved,—not verily
For their own sakes, but for the fields and hills   25

Where was their occupation and abode.
And hence this Tale, while I was yet a Boy
Careless of books, yet having felt the power
Of Nature, by the gentle agency
Of natural objects, led me on to feel   30
For passions that were not my own, and think
(At random and imperfectly indeed)
On man, the heart of man, and human life.
Therefore, although it be a history
Homely and rude, I will relate the same   35
For the delight of a few natural hearts;
And, with yet fonder feeling, for the sake   *Parallel with*
Of youthful Poets, who among these hills   *Michael*
Will be my second self when I am gone.

    Upon the forest-side in Grasmere Vale   40
There dwelt a Shepherd, Michael was his name;
An old man, stout of heart, and strong of limb.
His bodily frame had been from youth to age
Of an unusual strength: his mind was keen,
Intense, and frugal, apt for all affairs,   45
And in his shepherd's calling he was prompt
And watchful more than ordinary men.
Hence had he learned the meaning of all winds,
Of blasts of every tone; and oftentimes,
When others heeded not, he heard the South   50
Make subterraneous music, like the noise
Of bagpipers on distant Highland hills.
The Shepherd, at such warning, of his flock
Bethought him, and he to himself would say,
"The winds are now devising work for me!"   55
And, truly, at all times, the storm, that drives
The traveller to a shelter, summoned him
Up to the mountains: he had been alone
Amid the heart of many thousand mists,
That came to him, and left him, on the heights.   60

So lived he till his eightieth year was past.
And grossly that man errs, who should suppose
That the green valleys, and the streams and rocks,
Were things indifferent to the Shepherd's thoughts.
Fields, where with cheerful spirits he had breathed   65
The common air; hills, which with vigorous step
He had so often climbed; which had impressed
So many incidents upon his mind
Of hardship, skill or courage, joy or fear;
Which, like a book, preserved the memory   70
Of the dumb animals, whom he had saved,
Had fed or sheltered, linking to such acts
The certainty of honourable gain;
Those fields, those hills—what could they less? had laid
Strong hold on his affections, were to him   75
A pleasurable feeling of blind love,
The pleasure which there is in life itself.

His days had not been passed in singleness.
His Helpmate was a comely matron, old—
Though younger than himself full twenty years.   80
She was a woman of a stirring life,
Whose heart was in her house: two wheels she had
Of antique form; this large, for spinning wool;
That small, for flax; and, if one wheel had rest,
It was because the other was at work.   85
The Pair had but one inmate in their house,
An only Child, who had been born to them
When Michael, telling o'er his years, began
To deem that he was old,—in shepherd's phrase,
With one foot in the grave. This only Son,   90
With two brave sheep-dogs tried in many a storm,
The one of an inestimable worth,
Made all their household. I may truly say,
That they were as a proverb in the vale
For endless industry. When day was gone,   95

And from their occupations out of doors
The Son and Father were come home, even then,
Their labour did not cease; unless when all
Turned to the cleanly supper-board, and there,
Each with a mess of pottage and skimmed milk,   100
Sat round the basket piled with oaten cakes,
And their plain home-made cheese. Yet when the meal
Was ended, Luke (for so the Son was named)
And his old Father both betook themselves
To such convenient work as might employ   105
Their hands by the fire-side; perhaps to card
Wool for the Housewife's spindle, or repair
Some injury done to sickle, flail, or scythe,
Or other implement of house or field.

   Down from the ceiling, by the chimney's edge,   110
That in our ancient uncouth country style
With huge and black projection overbrowed
Large space beneath, as duly as the light
Of day grew dim the Housewife hung a lamp;
An aged utensil, which had performed   115
Service beyond all others of its kind.
Early at evening did it burn—and late,
Surviving comrade of uncounted hours,
Which, going by from year to year, had found,
And left, the couple neither gay perhaps   120
Nor cheerful, yet with objects and with hopes,
Living a life of eager industry.
And now, when Luke had reached his eighteenth year,
There by the light of this old lamp they sate,
Father and Son, while far into the night   125
The Housewife plied her own peculiar work,
Making the cottage through the silent hours
Murmur as with the sound of summer flies.
This light was famous in its neighbourhood,
And was a public symbol of the life   130

That thrifty Pair had lived. For, as it chanced,
Their cottage on a plot of rising ground
Stood single, with large prospect, north and south,
High into Easedale, up to Dunmail-Raise,
And westward to the village near the lake;   135
And from this constant light, so regular,
And so far seen, the House itself, by all
Who dwelt within the limits of the vale,
Both old and young, was named THE EVENING STAR.

Thus living on through such a length of years,   140
The Shepherd, if he loved himself, must needs
Have loved his Helpmate; but to Michael's heart
This son of his old age was yet more dear—
Less from instinctive tenderness, the same
Fond spirit that blindly works in the blood of all—   145
Than that a child, more than all other gifts
That earth can offer to declining man,
Brings hope with it, and forward-looking thoughts,
And stirrings of inquietude, when they
By tendency of nature needs must fail.   150
Exceeding was the love he bare to him,
His heart and his heart's joy! For oftentimes
Old Michael, while he was a babe in arms,
Had done him female service, not alone
For pastime and delight, as is the use   155
Of fathers, but with patient mind enforced
To acts of tenderness; and he had rocked
His cradle, as with a woman's gentle hand.

And in a later time, ere yet the Boy
Had put on boy's attire, did Michael love,   160
Albeit of a stern unbending mind,
To have the Young-one in his sight, when he
Wrought in the field, or on his shepherd's stool
Sate with a fettered sheep before him stretched

Under the large old oak, that near his door   165
Stood single, and, from matchless depth of shade,
Chosen for the Shearer's covert from the sun,
Thence in our rustic dialect was called
The CLIPPING TREE, a name which yet it bears,
There, while they two were sitting in the shade.   170
With others round them, earnest all and blithe,
Would Michael exercise his heart with looks
Of fond correction and reproof bestowed
Upon the Child, if he disturbed the sheep
By catching at their legs, or with his shouts   175
Scared them, while they lay still beneath the shears.

   And when by Heaven's good grace the boy grew up
A healthy Lad, and carried in his cheek
Two steady roses that were five years old;
Then Michael from a winter coppice cut   180
With his own hand a sapling, which he hooped
With iron, making it throughout in all
Due requisites a perfect shepherd's staff,
And gave it to the Boy; wherewith equipt
He as a watchman oftentimes was placed   185
At gate or gap, to stem or turn the flock;
And, to his office prematurely called,
There stood the urchin, as you will divine,
Something between a hindrance and a help;
And for this cause not always, I believe,   190
Receiving from his Father hire of praise;
Though nought was left undone which staff, or voice,
Or looks, or threatening gestures, could perform.

   But soon as Luke, full ten years old, could stand
Against the mountain blasts; and to the heights,   195
Not fearing toil, nor length of weary ways,
He with his Father daily went, and they
Were as companions, why should I relate

That objects which the Shepherd loved before
Were dearer now? that from the Boy there came   200
Feelings and emanations—things which were
Light to the sun and music to the wind;
And that the old Man's heart seemed born again?

    Thus in his Father's sight the Boy grew up:
And now, when he had reached his eighteenth year,   205
He was his comfort and his daily hope.

    While in this sort the simple household lived
From day to day, to Michael's ear there came
Distressful tidings. Long before the time
Of which I speak, the Shepherd had been bound   210
In surety for his brother's son, a man
Of an industrious life, and ample means;
But unforeseen misfortunes suddenly
Had prest upon him; and old Michael now
Was summoned to discharge the forfeiture,   215
A grievous penalty, but little less
Than half his substance. This unlooked-for claim,
At the first hearing, for a moment took
More hope out of his life than he supposed
That any old man ever could have lost.   220
As soon as he had armed himself with strength
To look his trouble in the face, it seemed
The Shepherd's sole resource to sell at once
A portion of his patrimonial fields.
Such was his first resolve; he thought again,   225
And his heart failed him. "Isabel", said he,
Two evenings after he had heard the news,
"I have been toiling more than seventy years,
And in the open sunshine of God's love
Have we all lived; yet, if these fields of ours   230
Should pass into a stranger's hand, I think
That I could not lie quiet in my grave.

Our lot is a hard lot; the sun himself
Has scarcely been more diligent than I;
And I have lived to be a fool at last   235
To my own family. An evil man
That was, and made an evil choice, if he
Were false to us; and, if he were not false,
There are ten thousand to whom loss like this
Had been no sorrow. I forgive him,—but   240
'Twere better to be dumb than to talk thus.

   "When I began, my purpose was to speak
Of remedies and of a cheerful hope.
Our Luke shall leave us, Isabel; the land
Shall not go from us, and it shall be free;   245
He shall possess it, free as is the wind
That passes over it. We have, thou know'st,
Another kinsman—he will be our friend
In this distress. He is a prosperous man,
Thriving in trade—and Luke to him shall go,   250
And with his kinsman's help and his own thrift
He quickly will repair this loss, and then
He may return to us. If here he stay,
What can be done? Where every one is poor,
What can be gained?"
                       At this the old Man paused,   255
And Isabel sat silent, for her mind
Was busy, looking back into past times.
There's Richard Bateman, thought she to herself,
He was a parish-boy—at the church-door
They made a gathering for him, shillings, pence,   260
And halfpennies, wherewith the neighbours bought
A basket, which they filled with pedlar's wares;
And, with this basket on his arm, the lad
Went up to London, found a master there,
Who, out of many, chose the trusty boy   265
To go and overlook his merchandise

Beyond the seas; where he grew wondrous rich,
And left estates and monies to the poor,
And, at his birth-place, built a chapel floored
With marble, which he sent from foreign lands.   270
These thoughts, and many others of like sort,
Passed quickly through the mind of Isabel,
And her face brightened. The old Man was glad,
And thus resumed:—"Well, Isabel! this scheme
These two days has been meat and drink to me.   275
Far more than we have lost is left us yet.
—We have enough—I wish indeed that I
Were younger;—but this hope is a good hope.
Make ready Luke's best garments, of the best
Buy for him more, and let us send him forth   280
Tomorrow, or the next day, or tonight;
If he *could* go, the Boy should go tonight."

Sooner started
the better

    Here Michael ceased, and to the fields went forth
With a light heart. The Housewife for five days
Was restless morn and night, and all day long   285
Wrought on with her best fingers to prepare
Things needful for the journey of her son.
But Isabel was glad when Sunday came
To stop her in her work: for, when she lay
By Michael's side, she through the last two nights   290
Heard him, how he was troubled in his sleep:
And when they rose at morning she could see
That all his hopes were gone. That day at noon
She said to Luke, while they two by themselves
Were sitting at the door, "Thou must not go: 295
We have no other Child but thee to lose,
None to remember—do not go away,
For if thou leave thy Father he will die."
The Youth made answer with a jocund voice;
And Isabel, when she had told her fears,   300
Recovered heart. That evening her best fare

Did she bring forth, and all together sat
Like happy people round a Christmas fire.

   With daylight Isabel resumed her work;
And all the ensuing week the house appeared   305
As cheerful as a grove in Spring: at length
The expected letter from their kinsman came,
With kind assurances that he would do
His utmost for the welfare of the Boy;
To which, requests were added, that forthwith   310
He might be sent to him. Ten times or more
The letter was read over; Isabel
Went forth to show it to the neighbours round;
Nor was there at that time on English land
A prouder heart than Luke's. When Isabel   315
Had to her house returned, the old Man said,
"He shall depart tomorrow". To this word
The Housewife answered, talking much of things
Which, if at such short notice he should go,
Would surely be forgotten. But at length   320
She gave consent, and Michael was at ease.

   Near the tumultuous brook of Greenhead Ghyll,
In that deep valley, Michael had designed
To build a Sheep-fold; and, before he heard
The tidings of his melancholy loss,   325
For this same purpose he had gathered up
A heap of stones, which by the streamlet's edge
Lay thrown together, ready for the work.
With Luke that evening thitherward he walked:
And soon as they had reached the place he stopped,   330
And thus the old Man spake to him:—"My son,
Tomorrow thou wilt leave me: with full heart
I look upon thee, for thou art the same
That wert a promise to me ere thy birth,
And all thy life hast been my daily joy.   335

I will relate to thee some little part
Of our two histories: 'twill do thee good
When thou art from me, even if I should touch
On things thou canst not know of.—After thou
First cam'st into the world—as oft befalls   340
To new-born infants—thou didst sleep away
Two days, and blessings from thy Father's tongue
Then fell upon thee. Day by day passed on,
And still I loved thee with increasing love.
Never to living ear came sweeter sounds   345
Than when I heard thee by our own fireside
First uttering, without words, a natural tune;
While thou, a feeding babe, didst in thy joy
Sing at thy Mother's breast. Month followed month,
And in the open fields my life was passed   350
And on the mountains; else I think that thou
Hadst been brought up upon thy Father's knees.
But we were playmates, Luke: among these hills,
As well thou knowest, in us the old and young
Have played together, nor with me didst thou   355
Lack any pleasure which a boy can know."
Luke had a manly heart; but at these words
He sobbed aloud. The old Man grasped his hand,
And said, "Nay, do not take it so—I see
That these are things of which I need not speak.   360
—Even to the utmost I have been to thee
A kind and a good Father: and herein
I but repay a gift which I myself
Received at others' hands; for, though now old
Beyond the common life of man, I still   365
Remember them who loved me in my youth.
Both of them sleep together: here they lived,
As all their Forefathers had done; and, when
At length their time was come, they were not loth
To give their bodies to the family mould.   370
I wished that thou shouldst live the life they lived,

But 'tis a long time to look back, my Son,
And see so little gain from threescore years.
These fields were burthened when they came to me;
Till I was forty years of age, not more   375
Than half of my inheritance was mine.
I toiled and toiled; God blessed me in my work,
And till these three weeks past the land was free.
—It looks as if it never could endure
Another Master. Heaven forgive me, Luke,   380
If I judge ill for thee, but it seems good
That thou shouldst go."
                              At this the old Man paused;
Then, pointing to the stones near which they stood,
Thus, after a short silence, he resumed:
"This was a work for us; and now, my Son,   385
It is a work for me. But, lay one stone—
Here, lay it for me, Luke, with thine own hands.
Nay, Boy, be of good hope;—we both may live
To see a better day. At eighty-four
I still am strong and hale;—do thou thy part;   390
I will do mine.—I will begin again
With many tasks that were resigned to thee:
Up to the heights, and in among the storms,
Will I without thee go again, and do
All works which I was wont to do alone,   395
Before I knew thy face.—Heaven bless thee, Boy!
Thy heart these two weeks has been beating fast
With many hopes; it should be so—yes—yes—
I knew that thou couldst never have a wish
To leave me, Luke: thou hast been bound to me   400
Only by links of love: when thou art gone,
What will be left to us!—But I forget
My purposes. Lay now the corner-stone,
As I requested; and hereafter, Luke,
When thou art gone away, should evil men   405
Be thy companions, think of me, my Son,

And of this moment; hither turn thy thoughts,
And God will strengthen thee: amid all fear
And all temptation, Luke, I pray that thou
May'st bear in mind the life thy Fathers lived,   410
Who, being innocent, did for that cause
Bestir them in good deeds. Now, fare thee well—
When thou return'st, thou in this place wilt see
A work which is not here: a covenant
'Twill be between us; but, whatever fate   415
Befall thee, I shall love thee to the last,
And bear thy memory with me to the grave."

    The Shepherd ended here; and Luke stooped down,
And, as his Father had requested, laid
The first stone of the Sheep-fold. At the sight   420
The old Man's grief broke from him; to his heart
He pressed his Son, he kissèd him and wept;
And to the house together they returned.
—Hushed was that House in peace, or seeming peace,
Ere the night fell:—with morrow's dawn the Boy   425
Began his journey, and, when he had reached
The public way, he put on a bold face;
And all the neighbours, as he passed their doors,
Came forth with wishes and with farewell prayers,
That followed him till he was out of sight.   430

    A good report did from their Kinsman come,
Of Luke and his well-doing: and the Boy
Wrote loving letters, full of wondrous news,
Which, as the Housewife phrased it, were throughout
"The prettiest letters that were ever seen".   435
Both parents read them with rejoicing hearts.
So, many months passed on: and once again
The Shepherd went about his daily work
With confident and cheerful thoughts; and now
Sometimes when he could find a leisure hour   440

He to that valley took his way, and there
Wrought at the Sheep-fold. Meantime Luke began
To slacken in his duty; and, at length,
He in the dissolute city gave himself
To evil courses: ignominy and shame   445
Fell on him, so that he was driven at last
To seek a hiding-place beyond the seas.

  There is a comfort in the strength of love;
'Twill make a thing endurable, which else
Would overset the brain, or break the heart: 450
I have conversed with more than one who well
Remember the old Man, and what he was
Years after he had heard this heavy news.
His bodily frame had been from youth to age
Of an unusual strength. Among the rocks   455
He went, and still looked up to sun and cloud,
And listened to the wind; and, as before,
Performed all kinds of labour for his sheep,
And for the land, his small inheritance.
And to that hollow dell from time to time   460
Did he repair, to build the Fold of which
His flock had need. 'Tis not forgotten yet
The pity which was then in every heart
For the old Man—and 'tis believed by all
That many and many a day he thither went,   465
And never lifted up a single stone.

  There, by the Sheep-fold, sometimes was he seen
Sitting alone, or with his faithful Dog,
Then old, beside him, lying at his feet.
The length of full seven years, from time to time,   470
He at the building of this Sheep-fold wrought,
And left the work unfinished when he died.
Three years, or little more, did Isabel
Survive her Husband: at her death the estate

Was sold, and went into a stranger's hand.   475
The Cottage which was named THE EVENING STAR
Is gone—the ploughshare has been through the ground
On which it stood; great changes have been wrought
In all the neighbourhood,—yet the oak is left
That grew beside their door; and the remains   480
Of the unfinished Sheep-fold may be seen
Beside the boisterous brook of Greenhead Ghyll.

ANDREW JONES

I hate that Andrew Jones: he'll breed
His children up to waste and pillage.
I wish the press-gang or the drum
Would, with its rattling music, come,
And sweep him from the village!

I said not this, because he loves
Through the long day to swear and tipple;
But for the poor dear sake of one
To whom a foul deed he had done,
A friendless Man, a travelling Cripple!

For this poor crawling helpless wretch
Some Horseman who was passing by,
A penny on the ground had thrown;
But the poor Cripple was alone
And could not stoop—no help was nigh.

Inch-thick the dust lay on the ground
For it had long been droughty weather;
So with his staff the Cripple wrought
Among the dust till he had brought
The halfpennies together.

It chanc'd that Andrew pass'd that way
Just at the time; and there he found
The Cripple in the mid-day heat
Standing alone, and at his feet
He saw the penny on the ground.

He stooped and took the penny up:
And when the Cripple nearer drew,
Quoth Andrew, "Under half-a-crown,
What a man finds is all his own,
And so, my Friend, good-day to you".

And *hence* I say, that Andrew's boys
Will all be train'd to waste and pillage;
And wish'd the press-gang, or the drum
Would, with its rattling music, come,
And sweep him from the village!

THE AFFLICTION OF MARGARET

I

Where art thou, my beloved Son,
Where art thou, worse to me than dead?
Oh find me, prosperous or undone!
Or, if the grave be now thy bed,
Why am I ignorant of the same
That I may rest; and neither blame
Nor sorrow may attend thy name?

II

Seven years, alas! to have received
No tidings of an only child;
To have despaired, have hoped, believed,
And been for evermore beguiled;
Sometimes with thoughts of very bliss!
I catch at them, and then I miss;
Was ever darkness like to this?

III

He was among the prime in worth,
An object beauteous to behold;
Well born, well bred; I sent him forth
Ingenuous, innocent, and bold:
If things ensued that wanted grace,
As hath been said, they were not base;
And never blush was on my face.

IV

Ah! little doth the young-one dream,
When full of play and childish cares,
What power is in his wildest scream,
Heard by his mother unawares!
He knows it not, he cannot guess:
Years to a mother bring distress;
But do not make her love the less.

V

Neglect me! no, I suffered long
From that ill thought; and, being blind,
Said, "Pride shall help me in my wrong:
Kind mother have I been, as kind
As ever breathed": and that is true;
I've wet my path with tears like dew,
Weeping for him when no one knew.

VI

My Son, if thou be humbled, poor,
Hopeless of honour and of gain,
Oh! do not dread thy mother's door;
Think not of me with grief and pain:
I now can see with better eyes;
And worldly grandeur I despise,
And fortune with her gifts and lies.

VII

Alas! the fowls of heaven have wings,
And blasts of heaven will aid their flight;
They mount—how short a voyage brings
The wanderers back to their delight!
Chains tie us down by land and sea;
And wishes, vain as mine, may be
All that is left to comfort thee.

VIII

Perhaps some dungeon hears thee groan,
Maimed, mangled by inhuman men;
Or thou upon a desert thrown
Inheritest the lion's den;
Or hast been summoned to the deep,
Thou, thou and all thy mates, to keep
An incommunicable sleep.

IX

I look for ghosts; but none will force
Their way to me: 'tis falsely said
That there was ever intercourse
Between the living and the dead;
For, surely, then I should have sight
Of him I wait for day and night,
With love and longings infinite.

X

My apprehensions come in crowds;
I dread the rustling of the grass;
The very shadows of the clouds
Have power to shake me as they pass:
I question things and do not find
One that will answer to my mind;
And all the world appears unkind.

XI

Beyond participation lie
My troubles, and beyond relief:
If any chance to heave a sigh,
They pity me, and not my grief.
Then come to me, my Son, or send
Some tidings that my woes may end;
I have no other earthly friend!

RESOLUTION AND INDEPENDENCE

I

There was a roaring in the wind all night;
The rain came heavily and fell in floods;
But now the sun is rising calm and bright;
The birds are singing in the distant woods;
Over his own sweet voice the Stock-dove broods;
The Jay makes answer as the Magpie chatters;
And all the air is filled with pleasant noise of waters.

II

All things that love the sun are out of doors;
The sky rejoices in the morning's birth;
The grass is bright with rain-drops,—on the moors
The hare is running races in her mirth;
And with her feet she from the plashy earth
Raises a mist; that, glittering in the sun,
Runs with her all the way, wherever she doth run.

III

I was a Traveller then upon the moor;
I saw the hare that raced about with joy;
I heard the woods and distant waters roar;
Or heard them not, as happy as a boy:
The pleasant season did my heart employ:
My old remembrances went from me wholly;
And all the ways of men, so vain and melancholy.

IV

But, as it sometimes chanceth, from the might
Of joy in minds that can no further go,
As high as we have mounted in delight
In our dejection do we sink as low;
To me that morning did it happen so;
And fears and fancies thick upon me came;
Dim sadness—and blind thoughts, I knew not, nor could name.

V

I heard the sky-lark warbling in the sky;
And I bethought me of the playful hare:
Even such a happy Child of earth am I;
Even as these blissful creatures do I fare;
Far from the world I walk, and from all care;
But there may come another day to me—
Solitude, pain of heart, distress, and poverty.

VI

My whole life I have lived in pleasant thought,
As if life's business were a summer mood;
As if all needful things would come unsought
To genial faith, still rich in genial good;
But how can he expect that others should
Build for him, sow for him, and at his call
Love him, who for himself will take no heed at all?

VII

I thought of Chatterton, the marvellous Boy,
The sleepless Soul that perished in his pride;
Of Him who walked in glory and in joy
Following his plough, along the mountain-side:
By our own spirits are we deified:
We Poets in our youth begin in gladness;
But thereof come in the end despondency and madness.

VIII

Now, whether it were by peculiar grace,
A leading from above, a something given,
Yet it befell that, in this lonely place,
When I with these untoward thoughts had striven,
Beside a pool bare to the eye of heaven
I saw a Man before me unawares:
The oldest man he seemed that ever wore grey hairs.

IX

As a huge stone is sometimes seen to lie
Couched on the bald top of an eminence;
Wonder to all who do the same espy,
By what means it could thither come, and whence;
So that it seems a thing endued with sense:
Like a sea-beast crawled forth, that on a shelf
Of rock or sand reposeth, there to sun itself;

X

Such seemed this Man, not all alive nor dead,
Nor all asleep—in his extreme old age:
His body was bent double, feet and head
Coming together in life's pilgrimage;
As if some dire constraint of pain, or rage
Of sickness felt by him in times long past,
A more than human weight upon his frame had cast.

XI

Himself he propped, limbs, body, and pale face,
Upon a long grey staff of shaven wood:
And, still as I drew near with gentle pace,
Upon the margin of that moorish flood
Motionless as a cloud the old Man stood,
That heareth not the loud winds when they call;
And moveth all together, if it move at all.

XII

At length, himself unsettling, he the pond
Stirred with his staff, and fixedly did look
Upon the muddy water, which he conned,
As if he had been reading in a book:
And now a stranger's privilege I took;
And, drawing to his side, to him did say,
"This morning gives us promise of a glorious day".

XIII

A gentle answer did the old Man make,
In courteous speech which forth he slowly drew:
And him with further words I thus bespake,
"What occupation do you there pursue?
This is a lonesome place for one like you".
Ere he replied, a flash of mild surprise
Broke from the sable orbs of his yet-vivid eyes.

XIV

His words came feebly, from a feeble chest,
But each in solemn order followed each,
With something of a lofty utterance drest—
Choice word and measured phrase, above the reach
Of ordinary men; a stately speech;
Such as grave Livers do in Scotland use,
Religious men, who give to God and man their dues.

XV

He told, that to these waters he had come
To gather leeches, being old and poor:
Employment hazardous and wearisome!
And he had many hardships to endure:
From pond to pond he roamed, from moor to moor;
Housing, with God's good help, by choice or chance;
And in this way he gained an honest maintenance.

XVI

The old Man still stood talking by my side;
But now his voice to me was like a stream
Scarce heard; nor word from word could I divide;
And the whole body of the Man did seem
Like one whom I had met with in a dream;
Or like a man from some far region sent,
To give me human strength, by apt admonishment.

XVII

My former thoughts returned: the fear that kills;
And hope that is unwilling to be fed;
Cold, pain, and labour, and all fleshly ills;
And mighty Poets in their misery dead.
—Perplexed, and longing to be comforted,
My question eagerly did I renew,
"How is it that you live, and what is it you do?"

XVIII

He with a smile did then his words repeat;
And said that, gathering leeches, far and wide
He travelled; stirring thus about his feet
The waters of the pools where they abide.
"Once I could meet with them on every side;
But they have dwindled long by slow decay;
Yet still I persevere, and find them where I may."

XIX

While he was talking thus, the lonely place,
The old Man's shape, and speech—all troubled me:
In my mind's eye I seemed to see him pace
About the weary moors continually,
Wandering about alone and silently.
While I these thoughts within myself pursued,
He, having made a pause, the same discourse renewed.

xx

And soon with this he other matter blended,
Cheerfully uttered, with demeanour kind,
But stately in the main; and, when he ended,
I could have laughed myself to scorn to find
In that decrepit Man so firm a mind.
"God", said I, "be my help and stay secure;
I'll think of the Leech-gatherer on the lonely moor!"

Sonnets

I   COMPOSED UPON WESTMINSTER BRIDGE, SEPTEMBER 3, 1802

Earth has not anything to show more fair:
Dull would he be of soul who could pass by
A sight so touching in its majesty:
This City now doth, like a garment, wear
The beauty of the morning; silent, bare,
Ships, towers, domes, theatres, and temples lie
Open unto the fields, and to the sky;
All bright and glittering in the smokeless air.
Never did sun more beautifully steep
In his first splendour, valley, rock, or hill;
Ne'er saw I, never felt, a calm so deep!
The river glideth at his own sweet will:
Dear God! the very houses seem asleep;
And all that mighty heart is lying still!

II

The world is too much with us; late and soon,
Getting and spending, we lay waste our powers:
Little we see in Nature that is ours;
We have given our hearts away, a sordid boon!
This Sea that bares her bosom to the moon;
The winds that will be howling at all hours,
And are up-gathered now like sleeping flowers;
For this, for everything, we are out of tune;
It moves us not.—Great God! I'd rather be
A Pagan suckled in a creed outworn;
So might I, standing on this pleasant lea,
Have glimpses that would make me less forlorn;
Have sight of Proteus rising from the sea;
Or hear old Triton blow his wreathèd horn.

III

Nuns fret not at their convent's narrow room;
And hermits are contented with their cells;
And students with their pensive citadels;
Maids at the wheel, the weaver at his loom,
Sit blithe and happy; bees that soar for bloom,
High as the highest Peak of Furness-fells,
Will murmur by the hour in foxglove bells:
In truth the prison, unto which we doom
Ourselves, no prison is: and hence for me,
In sundry moods, 'twas pastime to be bound
Within the Sonnet's scanty plot of ground;
Pleased if some Souls (for such there needs must be)
Who have felt the weight of too much liberty,
Should find brief solace there, as I have found.

IV

It is a beauteous evening, calm and free,
The holy time is quiet as a Nun
Breathless with adoration; the broad sun

F

Is sinking down in its tranquillity;
The gentleness of heaven broods o'er the Sea:
Listen! the mighty Being is awake,
And doth with his eternal motion make
A sound like thunder—everlastingly.
Dear Child! dear Girl! that walkest with me here,
If thou appear untouched by solemn thought,
Thy nature is not therefore less divine:
Thou liest in Abraham's bosom all the year;
And worshipp'st at the Temple's inner shrine,
God being with thee when we know it not.

v

Surprised by joy—impatient as the Wind
I turned to share the transport—Oh! with whom
But Thee, deep buried in the silent tomb,
That spot which no vicissitude can find?
Love, faithful love, recalled thee to my mind—
But how could I forget thee? Through what power,
Even for the least division of an hour,
Have I been so beguiled as to be blind
To my most grievous loss!—That thought's return
Was the worst pang that sorrow ever bore,
Save one, one only, when I stood forlorn,
Knowing my heart's best treasure was no more;
That neither present time, nor years unborn
Could to my sight that heavenly face restore.

VI   AFTER-THOUGHT

I thought of Thee, my partner and my guide,
As being past away.—Vain sympathies!
For, backward, Duddon! as I cast my eyes,
I see what was, and is, and will abide;
Still glides the Stream, and shall for ever glide;

The Form remains, the Function never dies;
While we, the brave, the mighty, and the wise,
We Men, who in our morn of youth defied
The elements, must vanish,—be it so!
Enough, if something from our hands have power
To live, and act, and serve the future hour;
And if, as toward the silent tomb we go,
Through love, through hope, and faith's transcendent dower,
We feel that we are greater than we know.

VII   LONDON, 1802

Milton! thou shouldst be living at this hour:
England hath need of thee: she is a fen
Of stagnant waters: altar, sword, and pen,
Fireside, the heroic wealth of hall and bower,
Have forfeited their ancient English dower
Of inward happiness. We are selfish men;
Oh! raise us up, return to us again;
And give us manners, virtue, freedom, power.
Thy soul was like a Star, and dwelt apart;
Thou hadst a voice whose sound was like the sea:
Pure as the naked heavens, majestic, free,
So didst thou travel on life's common way,
In cheerful godliness; and yet thy heart
The lowliest duties on herself did lay.

ALICE FELL

The post-boy drove with fierce career,
For threatening clouds the moon had drowned;
When, as we hurried on, my ear
Was smitten with a startling sound

As if the wind blew many ways,   5
I heard the sound,—and more and more;
It seemed to follow with the chaise,
And still I heard it as before.

At length I to the boy called out;
He stopped his horses at the word,   10
But neither cry, nor voice, nor shout,
Nor aught else like it, could be heard.

The boy then smacked his whip, and fast
The horses scampered through the rain;
But, hearing soon upon the blast   15
The cry, I bade him halt again.

Forthwith alighting on the ground,
"Whence comes", said I, "this piteous moan?"
And there a little Girl I found,
Sitting behind the chaise, alone.   20

"My cloak!" no other word she spake,
But loud and bitterly she wept,
As if her innocent heart would break;
And down from off her seat she leapt.

"What ails you, child?"—she sobbed, "Look there!"   25
I saw it in the wheel entangled,
A weather-beaten rag as e'er
From any garden scare-crow dangled.

There, twisted between nave and spoke,
It hung, nor could at once be freed;   30
But our joint pains unloosed the cloak,
A miserable rag indeed!

"And whither are you going, child,
Tonight along these lonesome ways?"
"To Durham", answered she, half wild—   35
"Then come with me into the chaise."

Insensible to all relief
Sat the poor girl, and forth did send
Sob after sob, as if her grief
Could never, never have an end.   40

"My child, in Durham do you dwell?"
She checked herself in her distress,
And said, "My name is Alice Fell;
I'm fatherless and motherless.

"And I to Durham, Sir, belong."   45
Again, as if the thought would choke
Her very heart, her grief grew strong;
And all was for her tattered cloak!

The chaise drove on; our journey's end
Was nigh; and, sitting by my side,   50
As if she had lost her only friend
She wept, nor would be pacified.

Up to the tavern-door we post;
Of Alice and her grief I told;
And I gave money to the host,   55
To buy a new cloak for the old.

"And let it be of duffil grey,
As warm a cloak as man can sell!"
Proud creature was she the next day,
The little orphan, Alice Fell!   60

TO THE CUCKOO

O blithe New-comer! I have heard,
I hear thee and rejoice.
O Cuckoo! shall I call thee Bird,
Or but a wandering Voice?

While I am lying on the grass
Thy twofold shout I hear;
From hill to hill it seems to pass
At once far off, and near.

Though babbling only to the Vale,
Of sunshine and of flowers,
Thou bringest unto me a tale
Of visionary hours.

Thrice welcome, darling of the Spring!
Even yet thou art to me
No bird, but an invisible thing,
A voice, a mystery;

The same whom in my schoolboy days
I listened to; that Cry
Which made me look a thousand ways
In bush, and tree, and sky.

To seek thee did I often rove
Through woods and on the green;
And thou wert still a hope, a love;
Still longed for, never seen.

And I can listen to thee yet;
Can lie upon the plain
And listen, till I do beget
That golden time again.

O blessèd Bird! the earth we pace
Again appears to be
An unsubstantial, faery place;
That is fit home for Thee!

THE SAILOR'S MOTHER

One morning (raw it was and wet—
A foggy day in winter time)
A Woman on the road I met,
Not old, though something past her prime:
Majestic in her person, tall and straight;
And like a Roman matron's was her mien and gait.

The ancient spirit is not dead;
Old times, thought I, are breathing there;
Proud was I that my country bred
Such strength, a dignity so fair:
She begged an alms, like one in poor estate;
I looked at her again, nor did my pride abate.

When from these lofty thoughts I woke,
"What is it", said I, "that you bear,
Beneath the covert of your Cloak,
Protected from this cold damp air?"
She answered, soon as she the question heard,
"A simple burthen, Sir, a little Singing-bird."

And, thus continuing, she said,
"I had a Son, who many a day
Sailed on the seas, but he is dead;
In Denmark he was cast away:
And I have travelled weary miles to see
If aught which he had owned might still remain for me.

"The bird and cage they both were his:
'Twas my Son's bird; and neat and trim
He kept it: many voyages
The singing-bird had gone with him;
When last he sailed, he left the bird behind;
From bodings, as might be, that hung upon his mind.

"He to a fellow-lodger's care
Had left it, to be watched and fed,
And pipe its song in safety,—there
I found it when my Son was dead;
And now, God help me for my little wit!
I bear it with me, Sir,—he took so much delight in it."

WRITTEN IN MARCH

WHILE RESTING ON THE BRIDGE AT THE FOOT OF BROTHER'S WATER

The Cock is crowing,
The stream is flowing,
The small birds twitter,
The lake doth glitter,
The green field sleeps in the sun;

The oldest and youngest
Are at work with the strongest;
The cattle are grazing,
Their heads never raising;
There are forty feeding like one!

Like an army defeated
The snow hath retreated,
And now doth fare ill
On the top of the bare hill;
The Ploughboy is whooping—anon—anon:
There's joy in the mountains;
There's life in the fountains;
Small clouds are sailing,
Blue sky prevailing;
The rain is over and gone!

ODE: INTIMATIONS OF IMMORTALITY FROM RECOLLECTIONS OF EARLY CHILDHOOD

The Child is father of the Man;
And I could wish my days to be
Bound each to each by natural piety.

I

There was a time when meadow, grove, and stream,
The earth, and every common sight,
    To me did seem
    Apparelled in celestial light,
The glory and the freshness of a dream.
It is not now as it hath been of yore,—
    Turn wheresoe'er I may,
    By night or day,
The things which I have seen I now can see no more.

II

The Rainbow comes and goes,
And lovely is the Rose,
The Moon doth with delight
Look round her when the heavens are bare,
Waters on a starry night
Are beautiful and fair;
The sunshine is a glorious birth;
But yet I know, where'er I go,
That there hath past away a glory from the earth.

III

Now, while the birds thus sing a joyous song,
And while the young lambs bound
As to the tabor's sound,
To me alone there came a thought of grief:
A timely utterance gave that thought relief,
And I again am strong:
The cataracts blow their trumpets from the steep;
No more shall grief of mine the season wrong;
I hear the Echoes through the mountains throng,
The Winds come to me from the fields of sleep,
And all the earth is gay;
Land and sea
Give themselves up to jollity,
And with the heart of May
Doth every Beast keep holiday,—
Thou Child of Joy,
Shout round me, let me hear thy shouts, thou happy
Shepherd-boy!

IV

Ye blessèd Creatures, I have heard the call
Ye to each other make; I see

The heavens laugh with you in your jubilee;
  My heart is at your festival,
  My head hath its coronal,
The fulness of your bliss, I feel—I feel it all.
    Oh evil day! if I were sullen
    While Earth herself is adorning,
      This sweet May-morning,
    And the Children are culling
      On every side,
    In a thousand valleys far and wide,
    Fresh flowers; while the sun shines warm,
And the Babe leaps up on his Mother's arm,—
    I hear, I hear, with joy I hear!
    —But there's a Tree, of many, one,
A single Field which I have looked upon,
Both of them speak of something that is gone:
    The Pansy at my feet
    Doth the same tale repeat:
Whither is fled the visionary gleam?
Where is it now, the glory and the dream?

          v

Our birth is but a sleep and a forgetting:
The Soul that rises with us, our life's Star,
    Hath had elsewhere its setting,
      And cometh from afar:
    Not in entire forgetfulness,
    And not in utter nakedness,
But trailing clouds of glory do we come
    From God, who is our home:
Heaven lies about us in our infancy!
Shades of the prison-house begin to close
    Upon the growing Boy
But He beholds the light, and whence it flows,
    He sees it in his joy;

The Youth, who daily farther from the east
Must travel, still is Nature's Priest,
And by the vision splendid
Is on his way attended;
At-length the Man perceives it die away,
And fade into the light of common day.

VI

Earth fills her lap with pleasures of her own;
Yearnings she hath in her own natural kind,
And, even with something of a Mother's mind,
And no unworthy aim,
The homely Nurse doth all she can
To make her Foster-child, her Inmate Man,
Forget the glories he hath known,
And that imperial palace whence he came.

VII

Behold the Child among his new-born blisses,
A six years' Darling of a pigmy size!
See, where 'mid work of his own hand he lies,
Fretted by sallies of his mother's kisses,
With light upon him from his father's eyes!
See, at his feet, some little plan or chart,
Some fragment from his dream of human life,
Shaped by himself with newly-learned art;
A wedding or a festival,
A mourning or a funeral;
And this hath now his heart,
And unto this he frames his song:
Then will he fit his tongue
To dialogues of business, love, or strife;
But it will not be long
Ere this be thrown aside,

    And with new joy and pride
The little Actor cons another part;
Filling from time to time his "humorous stage"
With all the Persons, down to palsied Age,
That Life brings with her in her equipage;
    As if his whole vocation
    Were endless imitation.

VIII

Thou, whose exterior semblance doth belie
    Thy Soul's immensity;
Thou best Philosopher, who yet dost keep
Thy heritage, thou Eye among the blind,
That, deaf and silent, read'st the eternal deep,
Haunted for ever by the eternal mind,—
    Mighty Prophet! Seer blest!
    On whom those truths do rest,
Which we are toiling all our lives to find,
In darkness lost, the darkness of the grave;
Thou, over whom thy Immortality
Broods like the Day, a Master o'er a Slave,
A Presence which is not to be put by;
    To whom the grave
Is but a lonely bed without the sense or sight
    Of day or the warm light,
A place of thought where we in waiting lie;
Thou little Child, yet glorious in the might
Of heaven-born freedom on thy being's height,
Why with such earnest pains dost thou provoke
The years to bring the inevitable yoke,
Thus blindly with thy blessedness at strife?
Full soon thy Soul shall have her earthly freight,
And custom lie upon thee with a weight,
Heavy as frost, and deep almost as life!

IX

O joy! that in our embers
Is something that doth live,
That nature yet remembers
What was so fugitive!
The thought of our past years in me doth breed
Perpetual benediction: not indeed
For that which is most worthy to be blest;
Delight and liberty, the simple creed
Of Childhood, whether busy or at rest,
With new-fledged hope still fluttering in his breast,—
Not for these I raise
The song of thanks and praise;
But for those obstinate questionings
Of sense and outward things,
Fallings from us, vanishings;
Blank misgivings of a Creature
Moving about in worlds not realized,
High instincts before which our mortal Nature
Did tremble like a guilty Thing surprised:
But for those first affections,
Those shadowy recollections,
Which, be they what they may,
Are yet the fountain-light of all our day,
Are yet a master-light of all our seeing;
Uphold us, cherish, and have power to make
Our noisy years seem moments in the being
Of the eternal Silence: truths that wake,
To perish never:
Which neither listlessness, nor mad endeavour,
Nor Man nor Boy,
Nor all that is at enmity with joy,
Can utterly abolish or destroy!
Hence in a season of calm weather
Though inland far we be,

Our Souls have sight of that immortal sea
   Which brought us hither,
  Can in a moment travel thither,
And see the Children sport upon the shore,
And hear the mighty waters rolling evermore.

X

Then sing, ye Birds, sing, sing a joyous song!
   And let the young Lambs bound
   As to the tabor's sound!
We in thought will join your throng,
   Ye that pipe and ye that play,
   Ye that through your hearts today
   Feel the gladness of the May!
What though the radiance which was once so bright
Be now for ever taken from my sight,
  Though nothing can bring back the hour
Of splendour in the grass, of glory in the flower;
   We will grieve not, rather find
   Strength in what remains behind;
   In the primal sympathy
   Which having been must ever be;
   In the soothing thoughts that spring
   Out of human suffering;
   In the faith that looks through death,
In years that bring the philosophic mind.

XI

And O, ye Fountains, Meadows, Hills, and Groves,
Forebode not any severing of our loves!
Yet in my heart of hearts I feel your might;
I only have relinquished one delight
To live beneath your more habitual sway.
I love the Brooks which down their channels fret,
Even more than when I tripped lightly as they;

The innocent brightness of a new-born Day
  Is lovely yet;
The Clouds that gather round the setting sun
Do take a sober colouring from an eye
That hath kept watch o'er man's mortality;
Another race hath been, and other palms are won.
Thanks to the human heart by which we live,
Thanks to its tenderness, its joys, and fears,
To me the meanest flower that blows can give
Thoughts that do often lie too deep for tears.

BEGGARS

She had a tall man's height or more;
Her face from summer's noontide heat
No bonnet shaded, but she wore
A mantle, to her very feet
Descending with a graceful flow,
And on her head a cap as white as new-fallen snow.

Her skin was of Egyptian brown:
Haughty, as if her eye had seen
Its own light to a distance thrown,
She towered, fit person for a Queen
To lead those ancient Amazonian files;
Or ruling Bandit's wife among the Grecian isles.

Advancing, forth she stretched her hand
And begged an alms with doleful plea
That ceased not; on our English land
Such woes, I knew, could never be;
And yet a boon I gave her, for the creature
Was beautiful to see—a weed of glorious feature.

I left her, and pursued my way;
And soon before me did espy
A pair of little Boys at play,
Chasing a crimson butterfly;
The taller followed with his hat in hand,
Wreathed round with yellow flowers the gayest of the land.

The other wore a rimless crown
With leaves of laurel stuck about;
And while both followed up and down,
Each whooping with a merry shout,
In their fraternal features I could trace
Unquestionable lines of that wild Suppliant's face.

Yet *they*, so blithe of heart, seemed fit
For finest tasks of earth or air:
Wings let them have, and they might flit
Precursors to Aurora's car,
Scattering fresh flowers; though happier far, I ween,
To hunt their fluttering game o'er rock and level green.

They dart across my path—but lo,
Each ready with a plaintive whine!
Said I, "Not half an hour ago
Your Mother has had alms of mine".
"That cannot be", one answered—"she is dead",—
I looked reproof—they saw—but neither hung his head.

"She has been dead, Sir, many a day."—
"Hush, boys! you're telling me a lie;
It was your Mother, as I say!"
And, in the twinkling of an eye,
"Come! come!" cried one, and without more ado
Off to some other play the joyous Vagrants flew!

I WANDERED LONELY AS A CLOUD

I wandered lonely as a cloud
That floats on high o'er vales and hills,
When all at once I saw a crowd,
A host, of golden daffodils;
Beside the lake, beneath the trees,
Fluttering and dancing in the breeze.

Continuous as the stars that shine
And twinkle on the milky way,
They stretched in never-ending line
Along the margin of a bay:
Ten thousand saw I at a glance,
Tossing their heads in sprightly dance.

The waves beside them danced; but they
Out-did the sparkling waves in glee:
A poet could not but be gay,
In such a jocund company:
I gazed—and gazed—but little thought
What wealth the show to me had brought.

For oft, when on my couch I lie
In vacant or in pensive mood,
They flash upon that inward eye
Which is the bliss of solitude;
And then my heart with pleasure fills,
And dances with the daffodils.

THE SOLITARY REAPER

Behold her, single in the field,
Yon solitary Highland Lass!
Reaping and singing by herself;
Stop here, or gently pass!
Alone she cuts and binds the grain,
And sings a melancholy strain;
O listen! for the Vale profound
Is overflowing with the sound.

No Nightingale did ever chaunt
More welcome notes to weary bands
Of travellers in some shady haunt,
Among Arabian sands:
A voice so thrilling ne'er was heard
In spring-time from the Cuckoo-bird,
Breaking the silence of the seas
Among the farthest Hebrides.

Will no one tell me what she sings?—
Perhaps the plaintive numbers flow
For old, unhappy, far off things,
And battles long ago:
Or is it some more humble lay,
Familiar matter of today?
Some natural sorrow, loss, or pain,
That has been, and may be again?

Whate'er the theme, the Maiden sang
As if her song could have no ending;
I saw her singing at her work,
And o'er the sickle bending,—

I listened, motionless and still;
And, as I mounted up the hill,
The music in my heart I bore,
Long after it was heard no more.

ELEGIAC STANZAS

SUGGESTED BY A PICTURE OF PEELE CASTLE, IN A STORM, PAINTED BY
SIR GEORGE BEAUMONT

I was thy neighbour once, thou rugged Pile!
Four summer weeks I dwelt in sight of thee:
I saw thee every day; and all the while
Thy Form was sleeping on a glassy sea.

So pure the sky, so quiet was the air!
So like, so very like, was day to day!
Whene'er I looked, thy Image still was there;
It trembled, but it never passed away.

How perfect was the calm! it seemed no sleep;
No mood, which season takes away, or brings:
I could have fancied that the mighty Deep
Was even the gentlest of all gentle Things.

Ah! then, if mine had been the Painter's hand,
To express what then I saw; and add the gleam,
The light that never was, on sea or land,
The consecration, and the Poet's dream;

I would have planted thee, thou hoary Pile
Amid a world how different from this!
Beside a sea that could not cease to smile;
On tranquil land, beneath a sky of bliss.

Thou shouldst have seemed a treasure-house divine
Of peaceful years; a chronicle of heaven,—
Of all the sunbeams that did ever shine
The very sweetest had to thee been given.

A Picture had it been of lasting ease,
Elysian quiet, without toil or strife;
No motion but the moving tide, a breeze,
Or merely silent Nature's breathing life.

Such, in the fond illusion of my heart,
Such Picture would I at that time have made:
And seen the soul of truth in every part,
A steadfast peace that might not be betrayed.

So once it would have been,—'tis so no more;
I have submitted to a new control:
A power is gone, which nothing can restore;
A deep distress hath humanized my Soul.

Not for a moment could I now behold
A smiling sea, and be what I have been:
The feeling of my loss will ne'er be old;
This, which I know, I speak with mind serene.

Then, Beaumont, Friend! who would have been the Friend,
If he had lived, of Him whom I deplore,
This work of thine I blame not, but commend;
This sea in anger, and that dismal shore.

O 'tis a passionate Work!—yet wise and well,
Well chosen is the spirit that is here;
That Hulk which labours in the deadly swell,
This rueful sky, this pageantry of fear!

And this huge Castle, standing here sublime,
I love to see the look with which it braves,
Cased in the unfeeling armour of old time,
The lightning, the fierce wind, and trampling waves.

Farewell, farewell the heart that lives alone,
Housed in a dream, at distance from the Kind!
Such happiness, wherever it be known,
Is to be pitied; for 'tis surely blind.

But welcome fortitude, and patient cheer,
And frequent sights of what is to be borne!
Such sights, or worse, as are before me here.—
Not without hope we suffer and we mourn.

CHARACTER OF THE HAPPY WARRIOR

Who is the happy Warrior? Who is he
That every man in arms should wish to be?
—It is the generous Spirit, who, when brought
Among the tasks of real life, hath wrought
Upon the plan that pleased his boyish thought: 5
Whose high endeavours are an inward light
That makes the path before him always bright;
Who, with a natural instinct to discern
What knowledge can perform, is diligent to learn;
Abides by this resolve, and stops not there,   10
But makes his moral being his prime care;
Who, doomed to go in company with Pain,
And Fear, and Bloodshed, miserable train!
Turns his necessity to glorious gain;
In face of these doth exercise a power   15
Which is our human nature's highest dower;
Controls them and subdues, transmutes, bereaves
Of their bad influence, and their good receives:
By objects, which might force the soul to abate
Her feeling, rendered more compassionate;   20
Is placable—because occasions rise
So often that demand such sacrifice;
More skilful in self-knowledge, even more pure,
As tempted more; more able to ensure,
As more exposed to suffering and distress;   25
Thence, also, more alive to tenderness.
—'Tis he whose law is reason; who depends
Upon that law as on the best of friends;
Whence, in a state where men are tempted still
To evil for a guard against worse ill,   30
And what in quality or act is best

Doth seldom on a right foundation rest.
He labours good on good to fix, and owes
To virtue every triumph that he knows:
—Who, if he rise to station of command,   35
Rises by open means; and there will stand
On honourable terms, or else retire,
And in himself possess his own desire;
Who comprehends his trust, and to the same
Keeps faithful with a singleness of aim;   40
And therefore does not stoop, nor lie in wait
For wealth, or honours, or for worldly state;
Whom they must follow; on whose head must fall,
Like showers of manna, if they come at all:
Whose powers shed round him in the common strife,   45
Or mild concerns of ordinary life,
A constant influence, a peculiar grace;
But who, if he be called upon to face
Some awful moment to which Heaven has joined
Great issues, good or bad for human kind,   50
Is happy as a Lover; and attired
With sudden brightness, like a Man inspired;
And, through the heat of conflict, keeps the law
In calmness made, and sees what he foresaw;
Or if an unexpected call succeed,   55
Come when it will, is equal to the need:
—He who, though thus endued as with a sense
And faculty for storm and turbulence,
Is yet a Soul whose master-bias leans
To homefelt pleasures and to gentle scenes;   60
Sweet images! which, wheresoe'er he be,
Are at his heart; and such fidelity
It is his darling passion to approve;
More brave for this, that he hath much to love,—
'Tis, finally, the Man, who, lifted high,   65
Conspicuous object in a Nation's eye,
Or left unthought-of in obscurity—

Who, with a toward or untoward lot,
Prosperous or adverse, to his wish or not—
Plays, in the many games óf life, that one   70
Where what he most doth value must be won:
Whom neither shape of danger can dismay,
Nor thought of tender happiness betray;
Who, not content that former worth stand fast,
Looks forward, persevering to the last,   75
From well to better, daily self-surpast:
Who, whether praise of him must walk the earth
For ever, and to noble deeds give birth,
Or he must fall, to sleep without his fame,
And leave a dead unprofitable name—   80
Finds comfort in himself and in his cause;
And, while the mortal mist is gathering, draws
His breath in confidence of Heaven's applause:
This is the happy Warrior; this is He
That every Man in arms should wish to be.   85

ODE TO DUTY

Stern Daughter of the Voice of God!
O Duty! if that name thou love
Who art a light to guide, a rod
To check the erring, and reprove;
Thou, who art victory and law
When empty terrors overawe;
From vain temptations dost set free;
And calm'st the weary strife of frail humanity!

There are who ask not if thine eye
Be on them; who, in love and truth,
Where no misgiving is, rely
Upon the genial sense of youth:
Glad Hearts! without reproach or blot;
Who do thy work, and know it not:
Oh! if through confidence misplaced
They fail, thy saving arms, dread Power! around them cast.

Serene will be our days and bright,
And happy will our nature be,
When love is an unerring light,
And joy its own security.
And they a blissful course may hold
Even now, who, not unwisely bold,
Live in the spirit of this creed;
Yet seek thy firm support, according to their need.

I, loving freedom, and untried;
No sport of every random gust,
Yet being to myself a guide,
Too blindly have reposed my trust:
And oft, when in my heart was heard
Thy timely mandate, I deferred
The task, in smoother walks to stray;
But thee I now would serve more strictly if I may.

Through no disturbance of my soul,
Or strong compunction in me wrought,
I supplicate for thy control;
But in the quietness of thought:
Me this unchartered freedom tires;
I feel the weight of chance-desires:
My hopes no more must change their name,
I long for a repose that ever is the same.

Stern Lawgiver! yet thou dost wear
The Godhead's most benignant grace;
Nor know we anything so fair
As is the smile upon thy face;
Flowers laugh before thee on their beds
And fragrance in thy footing treads;
Thou dost preserve the stars from wrong;
And the most ancient heavens, through
      Thee, are fresh and strong.

To humbler functions, awful Power!
I call thee: I myself commend
Unto thy guidance from this hour;
Oh, let my weakness have an end!
Give unto me, made lowly wise,
The spirit of self-sacrifice;
The confidence of reason give;
And in the light of truth thy Bondman let me live!

THE PRELUDE

CHILDHOOD I (FROM BOOK I)

Fair seed-time had my soul, and I grew up
Fostered alike by beauty and by fear:
Much favoured in my birthplace, and no less
In that belovèd Vale to which ere long
We were transplanted—there were we let loose   5
For sports of wider range. Ere I had told
Ten birth-days, when among the mountain-slopes
Frost, and the breath of frosty wind, had snapped
The last autumnal crocus, 'twas my joy
With store of springes o'er my shoulder hung   10
To range the open heights where woodcocks run
Among the smooth green turf. Through half the night,
Scudding away from snare to snare, I plied
That anxious visitation,—moon and stars
Were shining o'er my head. I was alone,   15
And seemed to be a trouble to the peace
That dwelt among them. Sometimes it befell
In these night wanderings, that a strong desire
O'erpowered my better reason, and the bird
Which was the captive of another's toil   20
Became my prey; and when the deed was done
I heard among the solitary hills
Low breathings coming after me, and sounds
Of undistinguishable motion, steps
Almost as silent as the turf they trod.   25

   Nor less when spring had warmed the cultured Vale,
Roved we as plunderers where the motherbird
Had in high places built her lodge; though mean

Our object and inglorious, yet the end
Was not ignoble. Oh! when I have hung   30
Above the raven's nest, by knots of grass
And half-inch fissures in the slippery rock
But ill sustained, and almost (so it seemed)
Suspended by the blast that blew amain,
Shouldering the naked crag, oh, at that time   35
While on the perilous ridge I hung alone,
With what strange utterance did the loud dry wind
Blow through my ear! the sky seemed not a sky
Of earth—and with what motion moved the clouds!

    Dust as we are, the immortal spirit grows   40
Like harmony in music; there is a dark
Inscrutable workmanship that reconciles
Discordant elements, makes them cling together
In one society. How strange that all
The terrors, pains, and early miseries,   45
Regrets, vexations, lassitudes interfused
Within my mind, should e'er have borne a part,
And that a needful part, in making up
The calm existence that is mine when I
Am worthy of myself! Praise to the end!   50
Thanks to the means which Nature deigned to employ;
Whether her fearless visitings, or those
That came with soft alarm, like hurtless light
Opening the peaceful clouds; or she may use
Severer interventions, ministry   55
More palpable, as best might suit her aim.

    One summer evening (led by her) I found
A little boat tied to a willow tree
Within a rocky cave, its usual home.
Straight I unloosed her chain, and stepping in   60
Pushed from the shore. It was an act of stealth
And troubled pleasure, nor without the voice

Of mountain-echoes did my boat move on;
Leaving behind her still, on either side,
Small circles glittering idly in the moon,   65
Until they melted all into one track
Of sparkling light. But now, like one who rows,
Proud of his skill, to reach a chosen point
With an unswerving line, I fixed my view
Upon the summit of a craggy ridge,   70
The horizon's utmost boundary; for above
Was nothing but the stars and the grey sky.
She was an elfin pinnace; lustily
I dipped my oars into the silent lake,
And, as I rose upon the stroke, my boat   75
Went heaving through the water like a swan;
When, from behind that craggy steep till then
The horizon's bound, a huge peak, black and huge,
As if with voluntary power instinct
Upreared its head. I struck and struck again,   80
And growing still in stature the grim shape
Towered up between me and the stars, and still,
For so it seemed, with purpose of its own
And measured motion like a living thing,
Strode after me. With trembling oars I turned,   85
And through the silent water stole my way
Back to the covert of the willow tree;
There in her mooring-place I left my bark,—
And through the meadows homeward went, in grave
And serious mood; but after I had seen   90
That spectacle, for many days, my brain
Worked with a dim and undetermined sense
Of unknown modes of being; o'er my thoughts
There hung a darkness, call it solitude
Or blank desertion. No familiar shapes   95
Remained, no pleasant images of trees,
Of sea or sky, no colours of green fields;
But huge and mighty forms, that do not live

Like living men, moved slowly through the mind
By day, and were a trouble to my dreams.   100

   Wisdom and Spirit of the universe!
Thou Soul that art the eternity of thought,
That givest to forms and images a breath
And everlasting motion, not in vain
By day or star-light thus from my first dawn   105
Of childhood didst thou intertwine for me
The passions that build up our human soul;
Not with the mean and vulgar works of man,
But with high objects, with enduring things—
With life and nature—purifying thus   110
The elements of feeling and of thought,
And sanctifying, by such discipline,
Both pain and fear, until we recognize
A grandeur in the beatings of the heart.
Nor was this fellowship vouchsafed to me   115
With stinted kindness. In November days,
When vapours rolling down the valley made
A lonely scene more lonesome, among woods,
At noon and 'mid the calm of summer nights,
When, by the margin of the trembling lake,   120
Beneath the gloomy hills homeward I went
In solitude, such intercourse was mine;
Mine was it in the fields both day and night,
And by the waters, all the summer long.

   And in the frosty season, when the sun   125
Was set, and visible for many a mile
The cottage windows blazed through twilight gloom,
I heeded not their summons: happy time
It was indeed for all of us—for me
It was a time of rapture! Clear and loud   130
The village clock tolled six,—I wheeled about,
Proud and exulting like an untired horse

That cares not for his home. All shod with steel,
We hissed along the polished ice in games
Confederate, imitative of the chase   135
And woodland pleasures,—the resounding horn,
The pack loud chiming, and the hunted hare.
So through the darkness and the cold we flew,
And not a voice was idle; with the din
Smitten, the precipices rang aloud;   140
The leafless trees and every icy crag
Tinkled like iron; while far distant hills
Into the tumult sent an alien sound
Of melancholy not unnoticed, while the stars
Eastward were sparkling clear, and in the west   145
The orange sky of evening died away.
Not seldom from the uproar I retired
Into a silent bay, or sportively
Glanced sideway, leaving the tumultuous throng,
To cut across the reflex of a star   150
That fled, and, flying still before me, gleamed
Upon the glassy plain; and oftentimes,
When we had given our bodies to the wind,
And all the shadowy banks on either side
Came sweeping through the darkness, spinning still   155
The rapid line of motion, then at once
Have I, reclining back upon my heels,
Stopped short; yet still the solitary cliffs
Wheeled by me—even as if the earth had rolled
With visible motion her diurnal round!   160
Behind me did they stretch in solemn train,
Feebler and feebler, and I stood and watched
Till all was tranquil as a dreamless sleep.

Ye Presences of Nature in the sky
And on the earth! Ye Visions of the hills!   165
And Souls of lonely places! can I think
A vulgar hope was yours when ye employed

Such ministry, when ye through many a year
Haunting me thus among my boyish sports,
On caves and trees, upon the woods and hills,   170
Impressed upon all forms the characters
Of danger or desire; and thus did make
The surface of the universal earth
With triumph and delight, with hope and fear,
Work like a sea?
            Not uselessly employed,   175
Might I pursue this theme through every change
Of exercise and play, to which the year
Did summon us in his delightful round.

  We were a noisy crew; the sun in heaven
Beheld not vales more beautiful than ours;   180
Nor saw a band in happiness and joy
Richer, or worthier of the ground they trod.
I could record with no reluctant voice
The woods of autumn, and their hazel bowers
With milk-white clusters hung; the rod and line,   185
True symbol of hope's foolishness, whose strong
And unreproved enchantment led us on
By rocks and pools shut out from every star,
All the green summer, to forlorn cascades
Among the windings hid of mountain brooks.   190
—Unfading recollections! at this hour
The heart is almost mine with which I felt,
From some hill-top on sunny afternoons,
The paper kite high among fleecy clouds
Pull at her rein like an impetuous courser;   195
Or, from the meadows sent on gusty days,
Beheld her breast the wind, then suddenly
Dashed headlong, and rejected by the storm.

  Ye lowly cottages wherein we dwelt,
A ministration of your own was yours;   200

G

Can I forget you, being as you were
So beautiful among the pleasant fields
In which ye stood? or can I here forget
The plain and seemly countenance with which
Ye dealt out your plain comforts? Yet had ye   205
Delights and exultations of your own.
Eager and never weary we pursued
Our home-amusements by the warm peat-fire
At evening, when with pencil, and smooth slate
In square divisions parcelled out and all   210
With crosses and with cyphers scribbled o'er,
We schemed and puzzled, head opposed to head
In strife too humble to be named in verse:
Or round the naked table, snow-white deal,
Cherry or maple, sate in close array,   215
And to the combat, Loo or Whist, led on
A thick-ribbed army; not, as in the world,
Neglected and ungratefully thrown by
Even for the very service they had wrought,
But husbanded through many a long campaign.   220
Uncouth assemblage was it, where no few
Had changed their functions; some, plebeian cards
Which Fate, beyond the promise of their birth,
Had dignified, and called to represent
The persons of departed potentates.   225
Oh, with what echoes on the board they fell!
Ironic diamonds,—clubs, hearts, diamonds, spades,
A congregation piteously akin!
Cheap matter offered they to boyish wit,
Those sooty knaves, precipitated down   230
With scoffs and taunts, like Vulcan out of heaven:
The paramount ace, a moon in her eclipse,
Queens gleaming through their splendour's last decay,
And monarchs surly at the wrongs sustained
By royal visages. Meanwhile abroad   235
Incessant rain was falling, or the frost

Raged bitterly, with keen and silent tooth;
And, interrupting oft that eager game,
From under Esthwaite's splitting fields of ice
The pent-up air, struggling to free itself,   240
Gave out to meadow-grounds and hills a loud
Protracted yelling, like the noise of wolves
Howling in troops along the Bothnic Main.

CHILDHOOD 2 (FROM BOOK II)

Midway on long Winander's eastern shore,
Within the crescent of a pleasant bay,
A tavern stood; no homely-featured house,
Primeval like its neighbouring cottages,
But 'twas a splendid place, the door beset   5
With chaises, grooms, and liveries, and within
Decanters, glasses, and the blood-red wine.
In ancient times, or ere the Hall was built
On the large island, had this dwelling been
More worthy of a poet's love, a hut,   10
Proud of its one bright fire and sycamore shade.
But—though the rhymes were gone that once inscribed
The threshold, and large golden characters,
Spread o'er the spangled sign-board, had dislodged
The old Lion and usurped his place, in slight   15
And mockery of the rustic painter's hand—
Yet, to this hour, the spot to me is dear
With all its foolish pomp. The garden lay
Upon a slope surmounted by a plain
Of a small bowling-green; beneath us stood   20
A grove, with gleams of water through the trees
And over the tree-tops; nor did we want
Refreshment, strawberries and mellow cream.
There, while through half an afternoon we played

On the smooth platform, whether skill prevailed   25
Or happy blunder triumphed, bursts of glee
Made all the mountains ring. But, ere nightfall,
When in our pinnace we returned at leisure
Over the shadowy lake, and to the beach
Of some small island steered our course with one,   30
The Minstrel of the Troop, and left him there,
And rowed off gently, while he blew his flute
Alone upon the rock—oh, then, the calm
And dead still water lay upon my mind
Even with a weight of pleasure, and the sky,   35
Never before so beautiful, sank down
Into my heart, and held me like a dream!
Thus were my sympathies enlarged, and thus
Daily the common range of visible things
Grew dear to me: already I began   40
To love the sun; a boy I loved the sun,
Not as I since have loved him, as a pledge
And surety of our earthly life, a light
Which we behold and feel we are alive;
Nor for his bounty to so many worlds—   45
But for this cause, that I had seen him lay
His beauty on the morning hills, had seen
The western mountain touch his setting orb,
In many a thoughtless hour, when, from excess
Of happiness, my blood appeared to flow   50
For its own pleasure, and I breathed with joy.
And, from like feelings, humble though intense,
To patriotic and domestic love
Analogous, the moon to me was dear;
For I could dream away my purposes,   55
Standing to gaze upon her while she hung
Midway between the hills, as if she knew
No other region, but belonged to thee,
Yea, appertained by a peculiar right
To thee and thy grey huts, thou one dear Vale!   60

Those incidental charms which first attached
My heart to rural objects, day by day
Grew weaker, and I hasten on to tell
How Nature, intervenient till this time
And secondary, now at length was sought   65
For her own sake. But who shall parcel out
His intellect by geometric rules,
Split like a province into round and square?
Who knows the individual hour in which
His habits were first sown, even as a seed?   70
Who that shall point as with a wand and say
"This portion of the river of my mind
Came from yon fountain?" Thou, my Friend! art one
More deeply read in thy own thoughts; to thee
Science appears but what in truth she is,   75
Not as our glory and our absolute boast,
But as a succedaneum, and a prop
To our infirmity. No officious slave
Art thou of that false secondary power
By which we multiply distinctions, then   80
Deem that our puny boundaries are things
That we perceive, and not that we have made.
To thee, unblinded by these formal arts,
The unity of all hath been revealed,
And thou wilt doubt, with me less aptly skilled   85
Than many are to range the faculties
In scale and order, class the cabinet
Of their sensations, and in voluble phrase
Run through the history and birth of each
As of a single independent thing.   90
Hard task, vain hope, to analyse the mind,
If each most obvious and particular thought,
Not in a mystical and idle sense,
But in the words of Reason deeply weighed,
Hath no beginning.
                    Blest the infant Babe,   95

(For with my best conjecture I would trace
Our Being's earthly progress,) blest the Babe,
Nursed in his Mother's arms, who sinks to sleep,
Rocked on his Mother's breast; who with his soul
Drinks in the feelings of his Mother's eye!   100
For him, in one dear Presence, there exists
A virtue which irradiates and exalts
Objects through widest intercourse of sense.
No outcast he, bewildered and depressed:
Along his infant veins are interfused   105
The gravitation and the filial bond
Of nature that connect him with the world.
Is there a flower, to which he points with hand
Too weak to gather it, already love
Drawn from love's purest earthly fount for him   110
Hath beautified that flower; already shades
Of pity cast from inward tenderness
Do fall around him upon aught that bears
Unsightly marks of violence or harm.
Emphatically such a Being lives,   115
Frail creature as he is, helpless as frail,
An inmate of this active universe:
For feeling has to him imparted power
That through the growing faculties of sense
Doth like an agent of the one great Mind   120
Create, creator and receiver both,
Working but in alliance with the works
Which it beholds.—Such, verily, is the first
Poetic spirit of our human life,
By uniform control of after years,   125
In most, abated or suppressed; in some,
Through every change of growth and of decay,
Pre-eminent till death.
                          From early days,
Beginning not long after that first time
In which, a Babe, by intercourse of touch   130

I held mute dialogues with my Mother's heart,
I have endeavoured to display the means
Whereby this infant sensibility,
Great birthright of our being, was in me
Augmented and sustained. Yet is a path   135
More difficult before me; and I fear
That in its broken windings we shall need
The chamois' sinews, and the eagle's wing:
For now a trouble came into my mind
From unknown causes. I was left alone   140
Seeking the visible world, nor knowing why.
The props of my affections were removed,
And yet the building stood, as if sustained
By its own spirit! All that I beheld
Was dear, and hence to finer influxes   145
The mind lay open, to a more exact
And close communion. Many are our joys
In youth, but oh! what happiness to live
When every hour brings palpable access
Of knowledge, when all knowledge is delight,   150
And sorrow is not there! The seasons came,
And every season wheresoe'er I moved
Unfolded transitory qualities,
Which, but for this most watchful power of love,
Had been neglected; left a register   155
Of permanent relations, else unknown.
Hence life, and change, and beauty, solitude
More active even than "best society"—
Society made sweet as solitude
By silent inobtrusive sympathies,   160
And gentle agitations of the mind
From manifold distinctions, difference
Perceived in things, where, to the unwatchful eye,
No difference is, and hence, from the same source,
Sublimer joy; for I would walk alone,   165
Under the quiet stars, and at that time

Have felt whate'er there is of power in sound
To breathe an elevated mood, by form
Or image unprofaned; and I would stand,
If the night blackened with a coming storm,   170
Beneath some rock, listening to notes that are
The ghostly language of the ancient earth,
Or make their dim abode in distant winds.
Thence did I drink the visionary power;
And deem not profitless those fleeting moods   175
Of shadowy exultation: not for this,
That they are kindred to our purer mind
And intellectual life; but that the soul,
Remembering how she felt, but what she felt
Remembering not, retains an obscure sense   180
Of possible sublimity, whereto
With growing faculties she doth aspire,
With faculties still growing, feeling still
That whatsoever point they gain, they yet
Have something to pursue.
                And not alone,   185
'Mid gloom and tumult, but no less 'mid fair
And tranquil scenes, that universal power
And fitness in the latent qualities
And essences of things, by which the mind
Is moved with feelings of delight, to me   190
Came strengthened with a superadded soul,
A virtue not its own. My morning walks
Were early;—often before the hours of school
I travelled round our little lake, five miles
Of pleasant wandering. Happy time! more dear   195
For this, that one was by my side, a Friend,
Then passionately loved; with heart how full
Would he peruse these lines! For many years
Have since flowed in between us, and our minds
Both silent to each other, at this time   200
We live as if those hours had never been.

Nor seldom did I lift our cottage latch
Far earlier, ere one smoke-wreath had risen
From human dwelling, or the vernal thrush
Was audible; and sate among the woods   205
Alone upon some jutting eminence,
At the first gleam of dawn-light, when the Vale,
Yet slumbering, lay in utter solitude.
How shall I seek the origin? where find
Faith in the marvellous things which then I felt?   210
Oft in these moments such a holy calm
Would overspread my soul, that bodily eyes
Were utterly forgotten, and what I saw
Appeared like something in myself, a dream,
A prospect in the mind.
                         'Twere long to tell   215
What spring and autumn, what the winter snows,
And what the summer shade, what day and night,
Evening and morning, sleep and waking thought,
From sources inexhaustible, poured forth
To feed the spirit of religious love   220
In which I walked with Nature. But let this
Be not forgotten, that I still retained
My first creative sensibility;
That by the regular action of the world
My soul was unsubdued. A plastic power   225
Abode with me; a forming hand, at times
Rebellious, acting in a devious mood;
A local spirit of his own, at war
With general tendency, but, for the most,
Subservient strictly to external things   230
With which it communed. An auxiliar light
Came from my mind, which on the setting sun
Bestowed new splendour; the melodious birds,
The fluttering breezes, fountains that run on
Murmuring so sweetly in themselves, obeyed   235
A like dominion, and the midnight storm

Grew darker in the presence of my eye:
Hence my obeisance, my devotion hence,
And hence my transport.
              Nor should this, perchance,
Pass unrecorded, that I still had loved   240
The exercise and produce of a toil,
Than analytic industry to me
More pleasing, and whose character I deem
Is more poetic as resembling more
Creative agency. The song would speak   245
Of that interminable building reared
By observation of affinities
In objects where no brotherhood exists
To passive minds. My seventeenth year was come;
And, whether from this habit rooted now   250
So deeply in my mind, or from excess
In the great social principle of life
Coercing all things into sympathy,
To unorganic natures were transferred
My own enjoyments; or the power of truth   255
Coming in revelation, did converse
With things that really are; I, at this time,
Saw blessings spread around me like a sea.
Thus while the days flew by, and years passed on,
From Nature and her overflowing soul   260
I had received so much, that all my thoughts
Were steeped in feeling; I was only then
Contented, when with bliss ineffable
I felt the sentiment of Being spread
O'er all that moves and all that seemeth still;   265
O'er all that, lost beyond the reach of thought
And human knowledge, to the human eye
Invisible, yet liveth to the heart;
O'er all that leaps and runs, and shouts and sings,
Or beats the gladsome air; o'er all that glides. 270
Beneath the wave, yea, in the wave itself,

And mighty depth of waters. Wonder not
If high the transport, great the joy I felt
Communing in this sort through earth and heaven
With every form of creature, as it looked 275
Towards the Uncreated with a countenance
Of adoration, with an eye of love.
One song they sang, and it was audible,
Most audible, then, when the fleshly ear,
O'ercome by humblest prelude of that strain, 280
Forgot her functions, and slept undisturbed.

THE THEME (FROM BOOK III)

Not of outward things
Done visibly for other minds, words, signs,
Symbols or actions, but of my own heart
Have I been speaking, and my youthful mind.
O Heavens! how awful is the might of souls, 5
And what they do within themselves while yet
The yoke of earth is new to them, the world
Nothing but a wild field where they were sown.
This is, in truth, heroic argument,
This genuine prowess, which I wished to touch 10
With hand however weak, but in the main
It lies far hidden from the reach of words.
Points have we all of us within our souls
Where all stand single; this I feel, and make
Breathings for incommunicable powers; 15
But is not each a memory to himself?—
And, therefore, now that we must quit this theme,
I am not heartless, for there's not a man
That lives who hath not known his godlike hours,
And feels not what an empire we inherit 20
As natural beings in the strength of Nature.

THE DISCHARGED SOLDIER (FROM BOOK IV)

Once, when those summer months
Were flown, and autumn brought its annual show
Of oars with oars contending, sails with sails,
Upon Winander's spacious breast, it chanced
That—after I had left a flower-decked room   5
(Whose in-door pastime, lighted up, survived
To a late hour), and spirits overwrought
Were making night do penance for a day
Spent in a round of strenuous idleness—
My homeward course led up a long ascent,   10
Where the road's watery surface, to the top
Of that sharp rising, glittered to the moon
And bore the semblance of another stream
Stealing with silent lapse to join the brook
That murmured in the vale. All else was still;   15
No living thing appeared in earth or air,
And, save the flowing water's peaceful voice,
Sound there was none—but, lo! an uncouth shape,
Shown by a sudden turning of the road,
So near that, slipping back into the shade   20
Of a thick hawthorn, I could mark him well,
Myself unseen. He was of stature tall,
A span above man's common measure, tall,
Stiff, lank, and upright; a more meagre man
Was never seen before by night or day.   25
Long were his arms, pallid his hands; his mouth
Looked ghastly in the moonlight: from behind,
A mile-stone propped him; I could also ken
That he was clothed in military garb,
Though faded, yet entire. Companionless,   30
No dog attending, by no staff sustained,
He stood, and in his very dress appeared
A desolation, a simplicity,

To which the trappings of a gaudy world
Make a strange back-ground. From his lips, ere long,   35
Issued low muttered sounds, as if of pain
Or some uneasy thought; yet still his form
Kept the same awful steadiness—at his feet
His shadow lay, and moved not. From self-blame
Not wholly free, I watched him thus; at length   40
Subduing my heart's specious cowardice,
I left the shady nook where I had stood
And hailed him. Slowly from his resting-place
He rose, and with a lean and wasted arm
In measured gesture lifted to his head   45
Returned my salutation; then resumed
His station as before; and when I asked
His history, the veteran, in reply,
Was neither slow nor eager; but, unmoved,
And with a quiet uncomplaining voice,   50
A stately air of mild indifference,
He told in few plain words a soldier's tale—
That in the Tropic Islands he had served,
Whence he had landed scarcely three weeks past;
That on his landing he had been dismissed,   55
And now was travelling towards his native home.
This heard, I said, in pity, "Come with me".
He stooped, and straightway from the ground took up
An oaken staff by me yet unobserved—
A staff which must have dropt from his slack hand   60
And lay till now neglected in the grass.
Though weak his step and cautious, he appeared
To travel without pain, and I beheld,
With an astonishment but ill suppressed,
His ghostly figure moving at my side;   65
Nor could I, while we journeyed thus, forbear
To turn from present hardships to the past,
And speak of war, battle, and pestilence,
Sprinkling this talk with questions, better spared,

On what he might himself have seen or felt.   70
He all the while was in demeanour calm,
Concise in answer; solemn and sublime
He might have seemed, but that in all he said
There was a strange half-absence, as of one
Knowing too well the importance of his theme,   75
But feeling it no longer. Our discourse
Soon ended, and together on we passed
In silence through a wood gloomy and still.
Up-turning, then, along an open field,
We reached a cottage. At the door I knocked,   80
And earnestly to charitable care
Commended him as a poor friendless man,
Belated and by sickness overcome.
Assured that now the traveller would repose
In comfort, I entreated that henceforth   85
He would not linger in the public ways,
But ask for timely furtherance and help
Such as his state required. At this reproof,
With the same ghastly mildness in his look,
He said, "My trust is in the God of Heaven,   90
And in the eye of him who passes me!"

    The cottage door was speedily unbarred,
And now the soldier touched his hat once more
With his lean hand, and in a faltering voice,
Whose tone bespake reviving interests   95
Till then unfelt, he thanked me; I returned
The farewell blessing of the patient man,
And so we parted. Back I cast a look,
And lingered near the door a little space,
Then sought with quiet heart my distant home.   100

CROSSING THE ALPS (FROM BOOK VI)

That very day,
From a bare ridge we also first beheld
Unveiled the summit of Mont Blanc, and grieved
To have a soulless image on the eye
That had usurped upon a living thought   5
That never more could be. The wondrous Vale
Of Chamouny stretched far below, and soon
With its dumb cataracts and streams of ice,
A motionless array of mighty waves,
Five rivers broad and vast, made rich amends,   10
And reconciled us to realities;
There small birds warble from the leafy trees,
The eagle soars high in the element,
There doth the reaper bind the yellow sheaf,
The maiden spread the haycock in the sun,   15
While Winter like a well-tamed lion walks,
Descending from the mountain to make sport
Among the cottages by beds of flowers.

    Whate'er in this wide circuit we beheld,
Or heard, was fitted to our unripe state   20
Of intellect and heart. With such a book
Before our eyes, we could not choose but read
Lessons of genuine brotherhood, the plain
And universal reason of mankind,
The truths of young and old. Nor, side by side   25
Pacing, two social pilgrims, or alone
Each with his humour, could we fail to abound
In dreams and fictions, pensively composed:
Dejection taken up for pleasure's sake,
And gilded sympathies, the willow wreath,   30
And sober posies of funereal flowers,
Gathered among those solitudes sublime

From formal gardens of the lady Sorrow,
Did sweeten many a meditative hour.

Yet still in me with those soft luxuries   35
Mixed something of stern mood, an under-thirst
Of vigour seldom utterly allayed:
And from that source how different a sadness
Would issue, let one incident make known.
When from the Vallais we had turned, and clomb   40
Along the Simplon's steep and rugged road,
Following a band of muleteers, we reached
A halting-place, where all together took
Their noon-tide meal. Hastily rose our guide,
Leaving us at the board; awhile we lingered,   45
Then paced the beaten downward way that led
Right to a rough stream's edge, and there broke off;
The only track now visible was one
That from the torrent's further brink held forth
Conspicuous invitation to ascend   50
A lofty mountain. After brief delay
Crossing the unbridged stream, that road we took,
And clomb with eagerness, till anxious fears
Intruded, for we failed to overtake
Our comrades gone before. By fortunate chance,   55
While every moment added doubt to doubt,
A peasant met us, from whose mouth we learned
That to the spot which had perplexed us first
We must descend, and there should find the road,
Which in the stony channel of the stream   60
Lay a few steps, and then along its banks;
And, that our future course, all plain to sight,
Was downwards, with the current of that stream.
Loth to believe what we so grieved to hear,
For still we had hopes that pointed to the clouds,   65
We questioned him again, and yet again;
But every word that from the peasant's lips

Came in reply, translated by our feelings,
Ended in this,—*that we had crossed the Alps.*

   Imagination—here the Power so called   70
Through sad incompetence of human speech,
That awful Power rose from the mind's abyss
Like an unfathered vapour that enwraps,
At once, some lonely traveller. I was lost;
Halted without an effort to break through;   75
But to my conscious soul I now can say—
"I recognize thy glory": in such strength
Of usurpation, when the light of sense
Goes out, but with a flash that has revealed
The invisible world, doth greatness make abode,   80
There harbours; whether we be young or old,
Our destiny, our being's heart and home,
Is with infinitude, and only there;
With hope it is, hope that can never die,
Effort, and expectation, and desire,   85
And something evermore about to be.
Under such banners militant, the soul
Seeks for no trophies, struggles for no spoils
That may attest her prowess, blest in thoughts
That are their own perfection and reward,   90
Strong in herself and in beatitude
That hides her, like the mighty flood of Nile
Poured from his fount of Abyssinian clouds
To fertilize the whole Egyptian plain.

   The melancholy slackening that ensued   95
Upon those tidings by the peasant given
Was soon dislodged. Downwards we hurried fast,
And, with the half-shaped road which we had missed,
Entered a narrow chasm. The brook and road
Were fellow-travellers in this gloomy strait,   100
And with them did we journey several hours

At a slow pace. The immeasurable height
Of woods decaying, never to be decayed,
The stationary blasts of waterfalls,
And in the narrow rent at every turn   105
Winds thwarting winds, bewildered and forlorn,
The torrents shooting from the clear blue sky,
The rocks that muttered close upon our ears,
Black drizzling crags that spake by the way-side
As if a voice were in them, the sick sight   110
And giddy prospect of the raving stream,
The unfettered clouds and region of the Heavens,
Tumult and peace, the darkness and the light—
Were all like workings of one mind, the features
Of the same face, blossoms upon one tree;   115
Characters of the great Apocalypse,
The types and symbols of Eternity,
Of first, and last, and midst, and without end.

That night our lodging was a house that stood
Alone, within the valley, at a point   120
Where, tumbling from aloft, a torrent swelled
The rapid stream whose margin we had trod;
A dreary mansion, large beyond all need,
With high and spacious rooms, deafened and stunned
By noise of waters, making innocent sleep   125
Lie melancholy among weary bones.

THE FRENCH REVOLUTION I (FROM BOOK X)

Twice had the trees let fall
Their leaves, as often Winter had put on
His hoary crown, since I had seen the surge
Beat against Albion's shore, since ear of mine
Had caught the accents of my native speech   5

Upon our native country's sacred ground.
A patriot of the world, how could I glide
Into communion with her sylvan shades,
Erewhile my tuneful haunt? It pleased me more
To abide in the great City, where I found   10
The general air still busy with the stir
Of that first memorable onset made
By a strong levy of humanity
Upon the traffickers in Negro blood;
Effort which, though defeated, had recalled   15
To notice old forgotten principles,
And through the nation spread a novel heat
Of virtuous feeling. For myself, I own
That this particular strife had wanted power
To rivet my affections; nor did now   20
Its unsuccessful issue much excite
My sorrow; for I brought with me the faith
That, if France prospered, good men would not long
Pay fruitless worship to humanity,
And this most rotten branch of human shame,   25
Object, so seemed it, of superfluous pains,
Would fall together with its parent tree.
What, then, were my emotions, when in arms
Britain put forth her freeborn strength in league,
Oh, pity and shame! with those confederate Powers!   30
Not in my single self alone I found,
But in the minds of all ingenuous youth,
Change and subversion from that hour. No shock
Given to my moral nature had I known
Down to that very moment; neither lapse   35
Nor turn of sentiment that might be named
A revolution, save at this one time;
All else was progress on the self-same path
On which, with a diversity of pace,
I had been travelling: this a stride at once   40
Into another region. As a light

And pliant harebell, swinging in the breeze
On some grey rock—its birthplace—so had I
Wantoned, fast rooted on the ancient tower
Of my belovèd country, wishing not   45
A happier fortune than to wither there:
Now was I from that pleasant station torn
And tossed about in whirlwind. I rejoiced,
Yea, afterwards—truth most painful to record!—
Exulted, in the triumph of my soul,   50
When Englishmen by thousands were o'erthrown,
Left without glory on the field, or driven,
Brave hearts! to shameful flight. It was a grief,—
Grief call it not, 'twas anything but that,—
A conflict of sensations without name,   55
Of which *he* only, who may love the sight
Of a village steeple, as I do, can judge,
When, in the congregation bending all
To their great Father, prayers were offered up,
Or praises for our country's victories;   60
And, 'mid the simple worshippers, perchance
I only, like an uninvited guest
Whom no one owned, sate silent, shall I add,
Fed on the day of vengeance yet to come.

THE FRENCH REVOLUTION 2 (FROM BOOK X)

In France, the men, who, for their desperate ends,
Had plucked up mercy by the roots, were glad
Of this new enemy. Tyrants, strong before
In wicked pleas, were strong as demons now;
And thus, on every side beset with foes,   5
The goaded land waxed mad; the crimes of few
Spread into madness of the many; blasts

From hell came sanctified like airs from heaven.
The sternness of the just, the faith of those
Who doubted not that Providence had times   10
Of vengeful retribution, theirs who throned
The human Understanding paramount
And made of that their God, the hopes of men
Who were content to barter short-lived pangs
For a paradise of ages, the blind rage   15
Of insolent tempers, the light vanity
Of intermeddlers, steady purposes
Of the suspicious, slips of the indiscreet,
And all the accidents of life were pressed
Into one service, busy with one work.   20
The Senate stood aghast, her prudence quenched,
Her wisdom stifled, and her justice scared,
Her frenzy only active to extol
Past outrages, and shape the way for new,
Which no one dared to oppose or mitigate.   25

   Domestic carnage now filled the whole year
With feast-days; old men from the chimney-nook,
The maiden from the bosom of her love,
The mother from the cradle of her babe,
The warrior from the field—all perished, all—   30
Friends, enemies, of all parties, ages, ranks,
Head after head, and never heads enough
For those that bade them fall. They found their joy,
They made it proudly, eager as a child,
(If like desires of innocent little ones   35
May with such heinous appetites be compared),
Pleased in some open field to exercise
A toy that mimics with revolving wings
The motion of a wind-mill; though the air
Do of itself blow fresh, and make the vanes   40
Spin in his eyesight, *that* contents him not,
But, with the plaything at arm's length, he sets

His front against the blast, and runs amain,
That it may whirl the faster.
                              Amid the depth
Of those enormities, even thinking minds   45
Forgot, at seasons, whence they had their being;
Forgot that such a sound was ever heard
As Liberty upon earth: yet all beneath
Her innocent authority was wrought,
Nor could have been, without her blessèd name.   50
The illustrious wife of Roland, in the hour
Of her composure, felt that agony,
And gave it vent in her last words. O Friend!
It was a lamentable time for man,
Whether a hope had e'er been his or not;   55
A woeful time for them whose hopes survived
The shock; most woeful for those few who still
Were flattered, and had trust in human kind:
They had the deepest feeling of the grief.
Meanwhile the Invaders fared as they deserved: 60
The Herculean Commonwealth had put forth her arms,
And throttled with an infant godhead's might
The snakes about her cradle; that was well,
And as it should be; yet no cure for them
Whose souls were sick with pain of what would be   65
Hereafter brought in charge against mankind.
Most melancholy at that time, O Friend!
Were my day-thoughts,—my nights were miserable;
Through months, through years, long after the last beat
Of those atrocities, the hour of sleep   70
To me came rarely charged with natural gifts,
Such ghastly visions had I of despair
And tyranny, and implements of death;
And innocent victims sinking under fear,
And momentary hope, and worn-out prayer,   75
Each in his separate cell, or penned in crowds
For sacrifice, and struggling with forced mirth

And levity in dungeons, where the dust
Was laid with tears. Then suddenly the scene
Changed, and the unbroken dream entangled me   80
In long orations, which I strove to plead
Before unjust tribunals,—with a voice
Labouring, a brain confounded, and a sense,
Death-like, of treacherous desertion, felt
In the last place of refuge—my own soul.   85

REJECTION OF REASON (FROM BOOK X, 1805 TEXT)

I had approach'd, like other Youth, the Shield
Of human nature from the golden side
And would have fought, even to the death, to attest
The quality of the metal which I saw.
What there is best in individual Man,   5
Of wise in passion, and sublime in power,
What there is strong and pure in household love,
Benevolent in small societies,
And great in large ones also, when call'd forth
By great occasions, these were things of which   10
I something knew, yet even these themselves,
Felt deeply, were not thoroughly understood
By Reason; nay, far from it, they were yet,
As cause was given me afterwards to learn,
Not proof against the injuries of the day,   15
Lodged only at the Sanctuary's door,
Not safe within its bosom. Thus prepared,
And with such general insight into evil,
And of the bounds which sever it from good,
As books and common intercourse with life   20
Must needs have given; to the noviciate mind,
When the world travels in a beaten road,
Guide faithful as is needed, I began

To think with fervour upon management
Of Nations, what it is and ought to be,   25
And how their worth depended on their Laws
And on the Constitution of the State.

    O pleasant exercise of hope and joy!
For great were the auxiliars which then stood
Upon our side, we who were strong in love;   30
Bliss was it in that dawn to be alive,
But to be young was very heaven: O times,
In which the meagre, stale, forbidding ways
Of custom, law, and statute took at once
The attraction of a Country in Romance;   35
When Reason seem'd the most to assert her rights
When most intent on making of herself
A prime Enchanter to assist the work,
Which then was going forwards in her name.
Not favour'd spots alone, but the whole earth   40
The beauty wore of promise, that which sets,
To take an image which was felt, no doubt,
Among the bowers of paradise itself,
The budding rose above the rose full blown.
What temper at the prospect did not wake   45
To happiness unthought of? The inert
Were rouz'd, and lively natures rapt away:
They who had fed their childhood upon dreams,
The Play-fellows of Fancy, who had made
All powers of swiftness, subtlety, and strength   50
Their ministers, used to stir in lordly wise
Among the grandest objects of the sense,
And deal with whatsoever they found there
As if they had within some lurking right
To wield it; they too, who, of gentle mood,   55
Had watch'd all gentle motions, and to these
Had fitted their own thoughts, schemers more mild,
And in the region of their peaceful selves,

Did now find helpers to their hearts' desire,
And stuff at hand, plastic as they could wish,   60
Were call'd upon to exercise their skill,
Not in Utopia, subterraneous Fields,
Or some secreted Island, Heaven knows where,
But in the very world which is the world
Of all of us, the place in which, in the end,   65
We find our happiness, or not at all.

    Why should I not confess that earth was then
To me what an inheritance new-fallen
Seems, when the first time visited, to one
Who thither comes to find in it his home?   70
He walks about and looks upon the place
With cordial transport, moulds it, and remoulds,
And is half pleased with things that are amiss,
'Twill be such joy to see them disappear.

    An active partisan, I thus convoked   75
From every object pleasant circumstance
To suit my ends; I moved among mankind
With genial feelings still predominant;
When erring, erring on the better part,
And in the kinder spirit; placable,   80
Indulgent oft-times to the worst desires
As on one side not uninform'd that men
See as it hath been taught them, and that time
Gives rights to error; on the other hand
That throwing off oppression must be work   85
As well of licence as of liberty;
And above all, for this was more than all,
Not caring if the wind did now and then
Blow keen upon an eminence that gave
Prospect so large into futurity,   90
In brief, a child of nature, as at first,
Diffusing only those affections wider

That from the cradle had grown up with me,
And losing, in no other way than light
Is lost in light, the weak in the more strong.   95

    In the main outline, such, it might be said,
Was my condition, till with open war
Britain opposed the Liberties of France;
This threw me first out of the pale of love;
Sour'd and corrupted upwards to the source   100
My sentiments, was not, as hitherto,
A swallowing up of lesser things in great;
But change of them into their opposites,
And thus a way was opened for mistakes
And false conclusions of the intellect,   105
As gross in their degree and in their kind
Far, far more dangerous. What had been a pride
Was now a shame; my likings and my loves
Ran in new channels, leaving old ones dry,
And hence a blow which, in maturer age,   110
Would but have touch'd the judgment struck more deep
Into sensations near the heart: meantime,
As from the first, wild theories were afloat,
Unto the subtleties of which, at least,
I had but lent a careless ear, assured   115
Of this, that time would soon set all things right,
Prove that the multitude had been oppressed,
And would be so no more.
                            But when events
Brought less encouragement, and unto these
The immediate proof of principles no more   120
Could be entrusted, while the events themselves,
Worn out in greatness, and in novelty,
Less occupied the mind, and sentiments
Could through my understanding's natural growth
No longer justify themselves through faith   125
Of inward consciousness, and hope that laid

Its hand upon its object, evidence
Safer, of universal application, such
As could not be impeach'd, was sought elsewhere.

   And now, become Oppressors in their turn,   130
Frenchmen had changed a war of self-defence
For one of conquest, losing sight of all
Which they had struggled for; and mounted up,
Openly, in the view of earth and heaven,
The scale of Liberty. I read her doom,   135
Vex'd inly somewhat, it is true, and sore;
But not dismay'd, nor taking to the shame
Of a false Prophet; but, rouz'd up I stuck
More firmly to old tenets, and to prove
Their temper, strained them more, and thus in heat   140
Of contest did opinions every day
Grow into consequence, till round my mind
They clung, as if they were the life of it.

   This was the time when all things tending fast
To depravation, the Philosophy   145
That promised to abstract the hopes of man
Out of his feelings, to be fix'd thenceforth
For ever in a purer element
Found ready welcome. Tempting region that
For Zeal to enter and refresh herself,   150
Where passions had the privilege to work,
And never hear the sound of their own names;
But, speaking more in charity, the dream
Was flattering to the young ingenuous mind
Pleas'd with extremes, and not the least with that   155
Which makes the human Reason's naked self
The object of its fervour. What delight!
How glorious! in self-knowledge and self-rule,
To look through all the frailties of the world,
And, with a resolute mastery shaking off   160

The accidents of nature, time, and place,
That make up the weak being of the past,
Build social freedom on its only basis,
The freedom of the individual mind,
Which, to the blind restraint of general laws   165
Superior, magisterially adopts
One guide, the light of circumstances, flash'd
Upon an independent intellect.

   For howsoe'er unsettled, never once
Had I thought ill of human kind, or been   170
Indifferent to its welfare, but, enflam'd
With thirst of a secure intelligence
And sick of other passion, I pursued
A higher nature, wish'd that Man should start
Out of the worm-like state in which he is,   175
And spread abroad the wings of Liberty,
Lord of himself, in undisturb'd delight—
A noble aspiration, yet I feel
The aspiration, but with other thoughts
And happier; for I was perplex'd and sought   180
To accomplish the transition by such means
As did not lie in nature, sacrificed
The exactness of a comprehensive mind
To scrupulous and microscopic views
That furnish'd out materials for a work   185
Of false imagination, placed beyond
The limits of experience and of truth.

   Enough, no doubt, the advocates themselves
Of ancient institutions had perform'd
To bring disgrace upon their very names,   190
Disgrace of which custom and written law
And sundry moral sentiments as props
And emanations of those institutes

Too justly bore a part. A veil had been
Uplifted; why deceive ourselves? 'Twas so,   195
'Twas even so, and sorrow for the Man
Who either had not eyes wherewith to see,
Or seeing hath forgotten. Let this pass,
Suffice it that a shock had then been given
To old opinions; and the minds of all men   200
Had felt it; that my mind was both let loose,
Let loose and goaded. After what hath been
Already said of patriotic love,
And hinted at in other sentiments
We need not linger long upon this theme.   205
This only may be said, that from the first
Having two natures in me, joy the one
The other melancholy, and withal
A happy man, and therefore bold to look
On painful things, slow, somewhat, too, and stern   210
In temperament, I took the knife in hand
And stopping not at parts less sensitive,
Endeavoured with my best of skill to probe
The living body of society
Even to the heart; I push'd without remorse   215
My speculations forward; yea, set foot
On Nature's holiest places. Time may come
When some dramatic Story may afford
Shapes livelier to convey to thee, my Friend,
What then I learn'd, or think I learn'd, of truth,   220
And the errors into which I was betray'd
By present objects, and by reasoning false
From the beginning, inasmuch as drawn
Out of a heart which had been turn'd aside
From nature by external accidents,   225
And which was thus confounded more and more,
Misguiding and misguided. Thus I fared,
Dragging all passions, notions, shapes of faith,
Like culprits to the bar, suspiciously

Calling the mind to establish in plain day   230
Her titles and her honours, now believing,
Now disbelieving, endlessly perplex'd
With impulse, motive, right and wrong, the ground
Of moral obligation, what the rule
And what the sanction, till, demanding *proof*,   235
And seeking it in everything, I lost
All feeling of conviction, and, in fine,
Sick, wearied out with contrarieties,
Yielded up moral questions in despair,
And for my future studies, as the sole   240
Employment of the enquiring faculty,
Turn'd towards mathematics, and their clear
And solid evidence—Ah! then it was
That Thou, most precious Friend! about this time
First known to me, didst lend a living help   245
To regulate my Soul, and then it was
That the belovèd Woman in whose sight
Those days were pass'd, now speaking in a voice
Of sudden admonition, like a brook
That does but cross a lonely road, and now   250
Seen, heard and felt, and caught at every turn,
Companion never lost through many a league,
Maintain'd for me a saving intercourse
With my true self; for, though impair'd and chang'd
Much, as it seem'd, I was no further chang'd   255
Than as a clouded, not a waning moon:
She, in the midst of all, preserv'd me still
A Poet, made me seek beneath that name
My office upon earth, and nowhere else,
And lastly, Nature's Self, by human love   260
Assisted, through the weary labyrinth
Conducted me again to open day,
Revived the feelings of my earlier life,
Gave me that strength and knowledge full of peace,
Enlarged, and never more to be disturb'd,   265

Which through the steps of our degeneracy,
All degradation of this age, hath still
Upheld me, and upholds me at this day
In the catastrophe (for so they dream,
And nothing less), when finally, to close   270
And rivet up the gains of France, a Pope
Is summon'd in to crown an Emperor;
This last opprobrium, when we see the dog
Returning to his vomit, when the sun
That rose in splendour, was alive, and moved   275
In exultation among living clouds
Hath put his function and his glory off,
And, turned into a gewgaw, a machine,
Sets like an opera phantom.

NATURE'S STRENGTH (FROM BOOK XI, 1805 TEXT)

Oh! soul of Nature, excellent and fair,
That didst rejoice with me, with whom I too
Rejoiced, through early youth before the winds
And powerful waters, and in lights and shades
That march'd and countermarch'd about the hills   5
In glorious apparition, now all eye
And now all ear; but ever with the heart
Employ'd, and the majestic intellect;
Oh! Soul of Nature! that dost overflow
With passion and with life, what feeble men   10
Walk on this earth! how feeble have I been
When thou wert in thy strength! Nor this through stroke
Of human suffering, such as justifies
Remissness and inaptitude of mind,
But through presumption, even in pleasure pleas'd   15
Unworthily, disliking here, and there,
Liking, by rules of mimic art transferr'd

To things above all art. ~~But~~ more, for this,
Although a strong infection of the age,
Was never much my habit, giving way   20
To a comparison of scene with scene
Bent overmuch on superficial things,
Pampering myself with meagre novelties
Of colour or proportion, to the moods
Of time or season, to the moral power   25
The affections, and the spirit of the place,
Less sensible. Nor only did the love
Of sitting thus in judgment interrupt
My deeper feelings, but another cause
More subtle and less easily explain'd   30
That almost seems inherent in the Creature,
Sensuous and intellectual as he is,
A twofold Frame of body and of mind;
The state to which I now allude was one
In which the eye was master of the heart,   35
When that which is in every stage of life
The most despotic of our senses gain'd
Such strength in me as often held my mind
In absolute dominion. Gladly here,
Entering upon abstruser argument,   40
Would I endeavour to unfold the means
Which Nature studiously employs to thwart
This tyranny, summons all the senses each
To counteract the other and themselves,
And makes them all, and the objects with which all   45
Are conversant, subservient in their turn
To the great ends of Liberty and Power.
But this is matter for another Song;
Here only let me add that my delights,
Such as they were, were sought insatiably,   50
Though 'twas a transport of the outward sense,
Not of the mind, vivid but not profound:
Yet was I often greedy in the chase,

And roam'd from hill to hill, from rock to rock,
Still craving combinations of new forms,   55
New pleasure, wider empire for the sight,
Proud of its own endowments, and rejoiced
To lay the inner faculties asleep.
Amid the turns and counter-turns, the strife
And various trials of our complex being,   60
As we grow up, such thraldom of that sense
Seems hard to shun; and yet I knew a Maid,
Who, young as I was then, conversed with things
In higher style, from Appetites like these
She, gentle Visitant, as well she might,   65
Was wholly free, far less did critic rules
Or barren intermeddling subtleties
Perplex her mind; but, wise as Women are
When genial circumstance hath favor'd them,
She welcom'd what was given, and craved no more.   70
Whatever scene was present to her eyes,
That was the best, to that she was attuned
Through her humility and lowliness,
And through a perfect happiness of soul
Whose variegated feelings were in this   75
Sisters, that they were each some new delight:
For she was Nature's inmate. Her the birds
And every flower she met with, could they but
Have known her, would have lov'd. Methought such charm
Of sweetness did her presence breathe around   80
That all the trees, and all the silent hills
And every thing she look'd on, should have had
An intimation how she bore herself
Towards them and to all creatures. God delights
In such a being; for her common thoughts   85
Are piety, her life is blessedness.

      Even like this Maid before I was call'd forth
From the retirement of my native hills

H

I lov'd whate'er I saw; nor lightly lov'd,
But fervently, did never dream of aught   90
More grand, more fair, more exquisitely fram'd
Than those few nooks to which my happy feet
Were limited. I had not at that time
Liv'd long enough, nor in the least survived
The first diviner influence of this world,   95
As it appears to unaccustom'd eyes;
I worshipp'd then among the depths of things
As my soul bade me; could I then take part
In aught but admiration, or be pleased
With any thing but humbleness and love;   100
I felt, and nothing else; I did not judge,
I never thought of judging, with the gift
Of all this glory fill'd and satisfi'd.
And afterwards, when through the gorgeous Alps
Roaming, I carried with me the same heart: 105
In truth, this degradation, howsoe'er
Induced, effect in whatsoe'er degree
Of custom, that prepares such wantonness
As makes the greatest things give way to least,
Or any other cause which hath been named;   110
Or lastly, aggravated by the times,
Which with their passionate sounds might often make
The milder minstrelsies of rural scenes
Inaudible, was transient; I had felt
Too forcibly, too early in my life,   115
Visitings of imaginative power
For this to last: I shook the habit off
Entirely and for ever, and again
In Nature's presence stood, as I stand now,
A sensitive, and a creative Soul.   120

There are in our existence spots of time,
Which with distinct pre-eminence retain
A vivifying Virtue, whence, depress'd

By false opinion and contentious thought,
Or aught of heavier or more deadly weight,   125
In trivial occupations, and the round
Of ordinary intercourse, our minds
Are nourished and invisibly repair'd,
A virtue by which pleasure is enhanced
That penetrates, enables us to mount   130
When high, more high, and lifts us up when fallen.
This efficacious spirit chiefly lurks
Among those passages of life in which
We have had deepest feeling that the mind
Is lord and master, and that outward sense   135
Is but the obedient servant of her will.
Such moments, worthy of all gratitude,
Are scatter'd everywhere, taking their date
From our first childhood: in our childhood even
Perhaps are most conspicuous. Life with me,   140
As far as memory can look back, is full
Of this beneficent influence. At a time
When scarcely (I was then not six years old)
My hand could hold a bridle, with proud hopes
I mounted, and we rode towards the hills: 145
We were a pair of Horsemen; honest James
Was with me, my encourager and guide.
We had not travell'd long, ere some mischance
Disjoin'd me from my Comrade, and, through fear
Dismounting, down the rough and stony Moor   150
I led my Horse, and stumbling on, at length
Came to a bottom, where in former times
A Murderer had been hung in iron chains.
The Gibbet-mast was moulder'd down, the bones
And iron case were gone; but on the turf,   155
Hard by, soon after that fell deed was wrought
Some unknown hand had carved the Murderer's name.
The monumental writing was engraven
In times long past, and still, from year to year,

By superstition of the neighbourhood,   160
The grass is clear'd away; and to this hour
The letters are all fresh and visible.
Faltering, and ignorant where I was, at length
I chanced to espy those characters inscribed
On the green sod: forthwith I left the spot   165
And, reascending the bare Common, saw
A naked Pool that lay beneath the hills,
The Beacon on the summit, and more near,
A Girl who bore a Pitcher on her head
And seem'd with difficult steps to force her way   170
Against the blowing wind. It was, in truth,
An ordinary sight; but I should need
Colours and words that are unknown to man
To paint the visionary dreariness
Which, while I look'd all round for my lost Guide,   175
Did at that time invest the naked Pool,
The Beacon on the lonely Eminence,
The Woman, and her garments vex'd and toss'd
By the strong wind. When, in a blessed season
With those two dear Ones, to my heart so dear,   180
When in the blessed time of early love,
Long afterwards, I roam'd about
In daily presence of this very scene,
Upon the naked pool and dreary crags,
And on the melancholy Beacon, fell   185
The spirit of pleasure and youth's golden gleam;
And think ye not with radiance more divine
From these remembrances, and from the power
They left behind? So feeling comes in aid
Of feeling, and diversity of strength   190
Attends us, if but once we have been strong.
Oh! mystery of Man, from what a depth
Proceed thy honours! I am lost, but see
In simple childhood something of the base
On which thy greatness stands, but this I feel,   195

That from thyself it is that thou must give,
Else never canst receive. The days gone by
Come back upon me from the dawn almost
Of life: the hiding-places of my power
Seem open; I approach, and then they close;   200
I see by glimpses now; when age comes on,
May scarcely see at all, and I would give,
While yet we may, as far as words can give,
A substance and a life to what I feel:
I would enshrine the spirit of the past   205
For future restoration.

THE IMAGINATION (FROM BOOK XIV)

It was a close, warm, breezeless summer night,
Wan, dull, and glaring, with a dripping fog
Low-hung and thick that covered all the sky;
But, undiscouraged, we began to climb
The mountain-side. The mist soon girt us round,   5
And, after ordinary travellers' talk
With our conductor, pensively we sank
Each into commerce with his private thoughts:
Thus did we breast the ascent, and by myself
Was nothing either seen or heard that checked   10
Those musings or diverted, save that once
The shepherd's lurcher, who, among the crags,
Had to his joy unearthed a hedgehog, teased
His coiled-up prey with barkings turbulent.
This small adventure, for even such it seemed   15
In that wild place and at the dead of night,
Being over and forgotten, on we wound
In silence as before. With forehead bent
Earthward, as if in opposition set
Against an enemy, I panted up   20
With eager pace, and no less eager thoughts.

Thus might we wear a midnight hour away,
Ascending at loose distance each from each,
And I, as chanced, the foremost of the band;
When at my feet the ground appeared to brighten,   25
And with a step or two seemed brighter still;
Nor was time given to ask or learn the cause,
For instantly a light upon the turf
Fell like a flash, and lo! as I looked up,
The Moon hung naked in a firmament   30
Of azure without cloud, and at my feet
Rested a silent sea of hoary mist.
A hundred hills their dusky backs upheaved
All over this still ocean; and beyond,
Far, far beyond, the solid vapours stretched,   35
In headlands, tongues, and promontory shapes,
Into the main Atlantic, that appeared
To dwindle, and give up his majesty,
Usurped upon far as the sight could reach.
Not so the ethereal vault; encroachment none   40
Was there, nor loss; only the inferior stars
Had disappeared, or shed a fainter light
In the clear presence of the full-orbed Moon,
Who, from her sovereign elevation, gazed
Upon the billowy ocean, as it lay   45
All meek and silent, save that through a rift—
Not distant from the shore whereon we stood,
A fixed, abysmal, gloomy, breathing-place—
Mounted the roar of waters, torrents, streams
Innumerable, roaring with one voice!   50
Heard over earth and sea, and, in that hour,
For so it seemed, felt by the starry heavens.

When into air had partially dissolved
That vision, given to spirits of the night
And three chance human wanderers, in calm thought   55
Reflected, it appeared to me the type

Of a majestic intellect, its acts
And its possessions, what it has and craves,
What in itself it is, and would become.
There I beheld the emblem of a mind   60
That feeds upon infinity, that broods
Over the dark abyss, intent to hear
Its voices issuing forth to silent light
In one continuous stream; a mind sustained
By recognitions of transcendent power,   65
In sense conducting to ideal form,
In soul of more than mortal privilege.
One function, above all, of such a mind
Had Nature shadowed there, by putting forth,
'Mid circumstances awful and sublime,   70
That mutual domination which she loves
To exert upon the face of outward things,
So moulded, joined, abstracted, so endowed
With interchangeable supremacy,
That men, least sensitive, see, hear, perceive,   75
And cannot choose but feel. The power, which all
Acknowledge when thus moved, which Nature thus
To bodily sense exhibits, is the express
Resemblance of that glorious faculty
That higher minds bear with them as their own.   80
This is the very spirit in which they deal
With the whole compass of the universe:
They from their native selves can send abroad
Kindred mutations; for themselves create
A like existence; and, whene'er it dawns   85
Created for them, catch it, or are caught
By its inevitable mastery,
Like angels stopped upon the wing by sound
Of harmony from Heaven's remotest spheres.
Them the enduring and the transient both   90
Serve to exalt; they build up greatest things
From least suggestions; ever on the watch,

Willing to work and to be wrought upon,
They need not extraordinary calls
To rouse them; in a world of life they live,   95
By sensible impressions not enthralled,
But by their quickening impulse made more prompt
To hold fit converse with the spiritual world,
And with the generations of mankind
Spread over time, past, present, and to come,   100
Age after age, till Time shall be no more.
Such minds are truly from the Deity,
For they are Powers; and hence the highest bliss
That flesh can know is theirs—the consciousness
Of Whom they are, habitually infused   105
Through every image and through every thought,
And all affections by communion raised
From earth to heaven, from human to divine;
Hence endless occupation for the Soul,
Whether discursive or intuitive;   110
Hence cheerfulness for acts of daily life,
Emotions which best foresight need not fear,
Most worthy then of trust when most intense.
Hence, amid ills that vex and wrongs that crush
Our hearts—if here the words of Holy Writ   115
May with fit reverence be applied—that peace
Which passeth understanding, that repose
In moral judgments which from this pure source
Must come, or will by man be sought in vain.

    Oh! who is he that hath his whole life long   120
Preserved, enlarged, this freedom in himself?
For this alone is genuine liberty:
Where is the favoured being who hath held
That course unchecked, unerring, and untired,
In one perpetual progress smooth and bright?—   125
A humbler destiny have we retraced,
And told of lapse and hesitating choice,

And backward wanderings along thorny ways:
Yet—compassed round by mountain solitudes,
Within whose solemn temple I received   130
My earliest visitations, careless then
Of what was given me; and which now I range,
A meditative, oft a suffering, man—
Do I declare—in accents which, from truth
Deriving cheerful confidence, shall blend   135
Their modulation with these vocal streams—
That, whatsoever falls my better mind,
Revolving with the accidents of life,
May have sustained, that, howsoe'er misled,
Never did I, in quest of right and wrong,   140
Tamper with conscience from a private aim;
Nor was in any public hope the dupe
Of selfish passions; nor did ever yield
Wilfully to mean cares or low pursuits,
But shrunk with apprehensive jealousy   145
From every combination which might aid
The tendency, too potent in itself,
Of use and custom to bow down the soul
Under a growing weight of vulgar sense,
And substitute a universe of death   150
For that which moves with light and life informed,
Actual, divine, and true. To fear and love,
To love as prime and chief, for there fear ends,
Be this ascribed; to early intercourse,
In presence of sublime or beautiful forms,   155
With the adverse principles of pain and joy—
Evil as one is rashly named by men
Who know not what they speak. By love subsists
All lasting grandeur, by pervading love;
That gone, we are as dust.—Behold the fields   160
In balmy spring-time full of rising flowers
And joyous creatures; see that pair, the lamb
And the lamb's mother, and their tender ways

Shall touch thee to the heart; thou callest this love,
And not inaptly so, for love it is,   165
Far as it carries thee. In some green bower
Rest, and be not alone, but have thou there
The One who is thy choice of all the world:
There linger, listening, gazing, with delight
Impassioned, but delight how pitiable!   170
Unless this love by a still higher love
Be hallowed, love that breathes not without awe;
Love that adores, but on the knees of prayer,
By heaven inspired; that frees from chains the soul,
Lifted, in union with the purest, best,   175
Of earth-born passions, on the wings of praise
Bearing a tribute to the Almighty's Throne.

       This spiritual Love acts not nor can exist
Without Imagination, which, in truth,
Is but another name for absolute power   180
And clearest insight, amplitude of mind,
And Reason in her most exalted mood.
This faculty hath been the feeding source
Of our long labour: we have traced the stream
From the blind cavern whence is faintly heard   185
Its natal murmur; followed it to light
And open day; accompanied its course
Among the ways of Nature, for a time
Lost sight of it bewildered and engulphed;
Then given it greeting as it rose once more   190
In strength, reflecting from its placid breast
The works of man and face of human life;
And lastly, from its progress have we drawn
Faith in life endless, the sustaining thought
Of human Being, Eternity, and God.   195

       Imagination having been our theme,
So also hath that intellectual Love,

For they are each in each, and cannot stand
Dividually.—Here must thou be, O Man!
Power to thyself; no Helper hast thou here;   200
Here keepest thou in singleness thy state:
No other can divide with thee this work:
No secondary hand can intervene
To fashion this ability; 'tis thine,
The prime and vital principle is thine   205
In the recesses of thy nature, far
From any reach of outward fellowship,
Else is not thine at all. But joy to him,
Oh, joy to him who here hath sown, hath laid
Here, the foundation of his future years!   210
For all that friendship, all that love can do,
All that a darling countenance can look
Or dear voice utter, to complete the man,
Perfect him, made imperfect in himself,
All shall be his: and he whose soul hath risen   215
Up to the height of feeling intellect
Shall want no humbler tenderness; his heart
Be tender as a nursing mother's heart;
Of female softness shall his life be full,
Of humble cares and delicate desires,   220
Mild interests and gentlest sympathies.

    Child of my parents! Sister of my soul!
Thanks in sincerest verse have been elsewhere
Poured out for all the early tenderness
Which I from thee imbibed: and 'tis most true   225
That later seasons owed to thee no less;
For, spite of thy sweet influence and the touch
Of kindred hands that opened out the springs
Of genial thought in childhood, and in spite
Of all that unassisted I had marked   230
In life or nature of those charms minute
That win their way into the heart by stealth,

Still, to the very going-out of youth,
I too exclusively esteemed *that* love,
And sought *that* beauty, which, as Milton sings,   235
Hath terror in it. Thou didst soften down
This over-sternness; but for thee, dear Friend!
My soul, too reckless of mild grace, had stood
In her original self too confident,
Retained too long a countenance severe;   240
A rock with torrents roaring, with the clouds
Familiar, and a favourite of the stars:
But thou didst plant its crevices with flowers,
Hang it with shrubs that twinkle in the breeze,
And teach the little birds to build their nests   245
And warble in its chambers. At a time
When Nature, destined to remain so long
Foremost in my affections, had fallen back
Into a second place, pleased to become
A handmaid to a nobler than herself,   250
When every day brought with it some new sense
Of exquisite regard for common things,
And all the earth was budding with these gifts
Of more refined humanity, thy breath,
Dear Sister! was a kind of gentler spring   255
That went before my steps. Thereafter came
One whom with thee friendship had early paired;
She came, no more a phantom to adorn
A moment, but an inmate of the heart,
And yet a spirit, there for me enshrined   260
To penetrate the lofty and the low;
Even as one essence of pervading light
Shines in the brightest of ten thousand stars,
And the meek worm that feeds her lonely lamp
Couched in the dewy grass.
                           With such a theme,   265
Coleridge! with this my argument, of thee
Shall I be silent? O capacious Soul!

Placed on this earth to love and understand,
And from thy presence shed the light of love,
Shall I be mute, ere thou be spoken of?   270
Thy kindred influence to my heart of hearts
Did also find its way. Thus fear relaxed
Her overweening grasp; thus thoughts and things
In the self-haunting spirit learned to take
More rational proportions; mystery,   275
The incumbent mystery of sense and soul,
Of life and death, time and eternity,
Admitted more habitually a mild
Interposition—a serene delight
In closelier gathering cares, such as become   280
A human creature, howsoe'er endowed,
Poet, or destined for a humbler name;
And so the deep enthusiastic joy,
The rapture of the hallelujah sent
From all that breathes and is, was chastened, stemmed   285
And balanced by pathetic truth, by trust
In hopeful reason, leaning on the stay
Of Providence; and in reverence for duty,
Here, if need be, struggling with storms, and there
Strewing in peace life's humblest ground with herbs,   290
At every season green, sweet at all hours.

NOTES

(Except for two sonnets, placed in their group, and the extracts from The Prelude, *the poems are printed in chronological order of composition.)*

p. 65 MARGARET, OR THE RUINED COTTAGE (THE EXCURSION, Book I, *ll.* 438–956). The genesis of this poem dates from 1795 when Wordsworth wrote the passage from "Nine tedious years . . ." to "Last human tenant of these ruined walls". This became "The Ruined Cottage" by 1797. By 1802 Wordsworth had absorbed it into Book I of *The Excursion.* Although the setting appears to be the Lake District, Wordsworth is thinking of Dorset and Somerset, where he resided in 1797. In a note to Isabella Fenwick (1843) he says that the Wanderer was an idea of what he fancied his own character would have been under similar circumstances. He based the character upon two originals, but particularly upon Patrick, a Scots pedlar who married a kinswoman of his wife, Mary. This pedlar possessed "strong and pure imagination", a tender heart, and some gift for literature. Margaret, he says, represents "the character possessed in common by many women whom it has been my happiness to know in humble life . . . several of the most touching things which she is represented as saying and doing are taken from actual observation of the distresses and trials under which different persons were suffering, some of them strangers to me, and others daily under my notice."

ll. 38–41 An allusion to classical elegies.

l. 87 *loom.* Country cottages of the time often possessed hand-looms.

l. 109 *And their place knew them not.* Cf. Psalm ciii, 16.

p. 80 THE OLD CUMBERLAND BEGGAR. Wordsworth wrote: "The class of Beggars, to which the Old Man here described belongs, will probably soon be extinct. It consisted of poor and mostly old and infirm persons, who confined themselves to a stated round in their neighbourhood, and had certain fixed days, on which, at different houses, they regularly received alms, sometimes in money, but mostly in provisions" (1800 edition).

ll. 144–9 Wordsworth is critical of official Poor Law policy on the ground that it eliminates the possibility of charity from one human being to another on the basis of love.

l. 175 *chartered.* licensed.

Lyrical Ballads

p. 86 SIMON LEE THE OLD HUNTSMAN.· Published in the *Lyrical Ballads*, 1798, this poem was based on a huntsman known to Wordsworth at Alfoxden. Wordsworth made numerous alterations to it after 1798, generally with the object of bringing out the contrast between Simon in youth and in age.

p. 89 THE IDIOT BOY. Published in the *Lyrical Ballads*, 1798. In his letter to John Wilson (June 1802) published in Philip Wayne's *Letters of William Wordsworth* (Oxford University Press, World's Classics series), p. 44, Wordsworth says much of interest and importance about this poem. In general, he argues that the subject is a legitimate one for poetry, since idiocy is as much a part of human nature as old age, maternity, and so forth. In his note to Isabella Fenwick he says: ". . . this long poem was composed in the groves of Alfoxden, almost extempore; not a word, I believe, being corrected, though one stanza was omitted. I mention this in gratitude to those happy moments, for, in truth, I never wrote anything with so much glee."

l. 338 *These fourteen years.* This implies that Wordsworth's poetical work began at fourteen (i.e. in 1784). In a note to "The Evening Walk", dictated to Isabella Fenwick, he says much the same.

p. 104 LINES COMPOSED A FEW MILES ABOVE TINTERN ABBEY. Published in the *Lyrical Ballads*, 1798. "I began it upon leaving Tintern, after crossing the Wye, and concluded it just as I was entering Bristol in the evening, after a ramble of four or five days, with my sister", says Wordsworth in his note to Isabella Fenwick. In 1800 he wrote: "I have not ventured to call this poem an Ode; but it was written with a hope that in the transitions, and the impassioned music of the versification would be found the principal requisites of that species of composition".

l. 2 *five long winters!* A visit Wordsworth made five years before, on foot, to his friend, Robert Jones.

l. 4 *inland murmur.* The river is not affected by the tides a few miles above Tintern.

p. 109 THE LAST OF THE FLOCK. Published in the *Lyrical Ballads*, 1798. There is more than an implication in this poem that the possession of property is associated with noble feelings and that Godwin, in his attack on property in *Political Justice*, was wrong. "The incident", says Wordsworth in a note to Isabella Fenwick, "occurred in the village of Holford, close by Alfoxden."

p. 113 HER EYES ARE WILD. Published in the *Lyrical Ballads*, 1798, as "The Mad Mother". Professor de Selincourt writes: "Legouis notes that the poem was written, in revulsion from Godwin's tenet that the feelings should be subservient to the intelligence, to show the pathos of unreasoning affection."

"The subject was reported to me by a lady of Bristol who had seen the poor creature", says Wordsworth in his note to Isabella Fenwick.

p. 116 THE COMPLAINT OF A FORSAKEN INDIAN WOMAN. Published in the *Lyrical Ballads*, 1798, and inspired by an incident in a book by Samuel Hearne which Wordsworth read at Alfoxden. Hearne tells of a woman left behind by her Indian companions. Though she caught up with them three times, she fell behind at last and presumably died. The subject, the powerful, simple feelings of human nature, is central to the *Lyrical Ballads*.

p. 119 NUTTING. Originally intended as part of *The Prelude*. It was written in Germany and recalled a typical boyhood experience.

p. 121 THERE WAS A BOY. Incorporated in *The Prelude*, Book V, *ll.* 389–422.

p. 123 LUCY POEMS, 1799. "Strange fits of passion." The "Lucy" of this and the four following poems has been the subject of much speculation. Lucy was probably the poet's sister Dorothy. "She dwelt among the untrodden ways". Written in Goslar in the company of Dorothy. The river Dove could be any one of three known to Wordsworth. "I travelled among unknown men". Written after Wordsworth's return from Germany in 1799. "Three years she grew". "1799. Composed in the Hartz Forest." Note to Isabella Fenwick. "A slumber did my spirit seal". Coleridge wrote of this poem to Thomas Poole: "Some months ago Wordsworth transmitted to me a sublime epitaph. Whether it had any reality I cannot say. Most probably, in some gloomier moment he had fancied the moment in which his sister might die."

p. 127 RUTH. "Written in Germany 1799. Suggested by an account I had of a wanderer in Somersetshire." Wordsworth's note to Isabella Fenwick. Wordsworth had read Bartram's *Travels through North and South Carolina, Georgia, etc* and took from it his reference to the flora of Georgian scenery.

  l. 21 *With splendid feathers drest*. Taken from the frontispiece to Bartram's book (a portrait of a chieftain).

  ll. 55–7 This refers to the *gordonia lacianthus*, a plant that changed its colour from green to yellow to scarlet and lastly to purple.

  l. 60 Bartram describes the plant in his book thus: "Its thick foliage of a dark green colour is flowered over with large, milk-white fragrant blossoms . . . renewed every morning."

l. 64 flowers that with one scarlet gleam. Bartram describes the splendid appearance of these scarlet flowers scattered over the hills of the southern parts of America.

l. 214 Tone. A river in Somerset near the Quantock Hills.

p. 136 MICHAEL. Of this poem Wordsworth wrote to Thomas Poole on 8 April 1801: "I have attempted to give a picture of a man, of strong mind and lively sensibility, agitated by two of the most powerful affections of the human heart, the parental affection, and the love of . . . *landed* property, including the feelings of inheritance, home and personal and family independence. . . ." Wordsworth told Mr. Justice Coleridge in 1836 that "Michael was founded on the son of an old couple having become dissolute and run away from his parents; and on an old shepherd having been seven years in building up a sheepfold in a solitary valley".

l. 40 forest-side. Professor de Selincourt notes that this refers to the eastern side of the lake, between Greenhead Ghyll and Town End and that a house stands there named Forest Side.

l. 324 Sheep-fold. Wordsworth noted in his 1802 edition that a sheep-fold was an unroofed stone building placed near a brook for sheep-washing.

p. 152 THE AFFLICTION OF MARGARET. The story is based on that of a poor widow who lived in Penrith. "She kept a shop, and when she saw a stranger passing by, she was in the habit of going into the street to enquire of him after her son." Note to Isabella Fenwick.

p. 155 RESOLUTION AND INDEPENDENCE. "This old man", says Wordsworth in a note to Isabella Fenwick, "I met a few hundred yards from my cottage at Town-End, Grasmere; and the account of him is taken from his own mouth. I was in the state of feeling described in the beginning of the poem, while crossing over Barton Fell from Mr. Clarkson's, at the foot of Ullswater, towards Askam. The image of the hare I then observed on the ridge of the fell."

Writing about this poem to some friends, Wordsworth said of the leech-gatherer: "How came he here? thought I, or what can he be doing? I then describe him, whether ill or well is not for me to judge . . . but this I *can* affirm that . . . I cannot conceive a figure more impressive than that of an old man like this, the survivor of a wife and ten children, travelling alone among the mountains and all lonely places, carrying with him his own fortitude . . . ."

NOTES 243

l. 43 *I thought of Chatterton.* This poem is written in the metre of Chatterton's "Excellent Ballad of Charitie" which deals with a similar theme.

Sonnets

Wordsworth particularly admired the sonnets of Milton. In a note to Isabella Fenwick he observed: "Many years ago my sister happened to read to me the sonnets of Milton which I could at that time repeat; but somehow or other I was singularly struck with the style of harmony, and the gravity, and republican austerity of these compositions."

p. 160 COMPOSED UPON WESTMINSTER BRIDGE, SEPTEMBER 3, 1802. "Written on the roof of a coach, on my way to France", says Wordsworth in his note to Isabella Fenwick. Dorothy describes the scene in her *Journal* thus: "A beautiful morning. The city, St. Paul's, with the river—a multitude of little boats made a beautiful sight as we crossed Westminster Bridge; the houses not overhung by their clouds of smoke, and were hung out endlessly; yet the sun shone so brightly, with such a pure light, that there was something like the purity of one of Nature's own grand spectacles."

p. 161 "THE WORLD IS TOO MUCH WITH US."

l. 11 *this pleasant lea.* Taken from Spenser's "Colin Clout's Come Home Again", *l.* 283: "Yet seemed to be a goodly pleasant lea".

l. 13 *Proteus rising from the sea.* An echo of Milton, *Paradise Lost*, Book III, *ll.* 603–4.

l. 14 *Triton blow his wreathèd horn.* From "Colin Clout's Come Home Again", *l.* 245.

p. 161 "IT IS A BEAUTEOUS EVENING." "This was composed on the beach near Calais in the autumn of 1802", Wordsworth told Isabella Fenwick.

l. 9 *Dear Child.* Caroline, his daughter by Annette Vallon. Dorothy describes in her *Grasmere Journal* how she and William met Annette and Caroline in Calais on 31 July 1802: "We walked by the seashore almost every evening with Annette and Caroline, or him and I alone."

p. 162 "SURPRISED BY JOY" refers to Wordsworth's daughter Catherine, who died on 4 June 1812.

p. 162 AFTER-THOUGHT is the last and the best of Wordsworth's sonnet sequence entitled *The River Duddon, A Series of Sonnets.*

l. 7 This line appears as line 5 of Wordsworth's translation of Moschus's "Lament for Dion": "But we, the great, the mighty, and the wise".

l. 14 *We feel that* . . . Echo of Milton's "And feel that I am happier than I know" (*Paradise Lost*, Book VIII, *l.* 282).

p. 163 ALICE FELL. In Dorothy's *Grasmere Journal* for 16 February 1802 we read: "Mr. Graham said he wished William had been with him the other day—he was riding in a post-chaise and he heard a strange cry that he could not understand, the sound continued, and he called to the chaise driver to stop. It was a little girl that was crying as if her heart would burst. She had got up behind the chaise, and her cloak had been caught by the wheel, and was jammed in, and it hung there. She was crying after it. Poor thing." Even after being taken into the chaise the girl continued wretched.

l. 57 *duffil.* A cloth named after Duffel, in Brabant; a coarse woollen cloth with a thick nap.

p. 167 THE SAILOR'S MOTHER. "I met this woman near the Wishing-Gate, on the high-road that then led from Grasmere to Ambleside. Her appearance was exactly as here described, and such was her account, nearly to the letter", Wordsworth told Isabella Fenwick.

p. 168 WRITTEN IN MARCH WHILE RESTING ON THE BRIDGE AT THE FOOT OF BROTHER'S WATER. Composed in April, not March 1802. Dorothy describes the occasion thus: "When I returned I found William writing a poem descriptive of the sights and sounds we saw and heard. There was the gentle flowing of the stream, the glittering, lively lake, green fields, without a living creature to be seen on them; behind us, a flat pasture with forty-two cattle feeding . . . people were at work, ploughing, harrowing, and sowing . . . a dog barking now and then . . . cocks crowing, birds twittering; the snow in patches at the tops of the highest hills. . . ." Friday, 16 April (Good Friday) 1802.

p. 169 ODE: INTIMATIONS OF IMMORTALITY. Some difference of opinion exists about the exact date of composition of this poem but it seems certain that it was commenced in March 1802 and finished in the spring of 1804. Wordsworth's note to Isabella Fenwick is frequently quoted in regard to this poem. Some significant sentences run: "Nothing was more difficult for me in childhood than to admit the notion of death as a state applicable to my own being . . . I used to brood over the stories of Enoch and Elijah, and almost persuade myself that, whatever might become of others, I should be translated, in something of the same way, to heaven. With a feeling congenial to this, I was often unable to think of external things as having external existence, and I communed with all that I saw as something not apart from, but inherent in, my own immaterial nature. Many times while going to school have I grasped at a wall or tree to recall myself from this abyss of idealism to the reality." Wordsworth observes that such feelings cannot be peculiar to him but must be experienced by many others in childhood. He wrote to Mrs. Clarkson (December 1814): "A Reader who has not a vivid recollection of these feelings having existed in his mind cannot understand the poem."

ll. 1–6 The interesting metrical arrangement of these lines owes something to Coleridge's "Mad Monk".

l. 23 *A timely utterance.* Possibly the Rainbow poem ("My heart leaps up . . . "), written the day before the Ode was begun.

ll. 36–76 Professor de Selincourt observes that there are clear parallels between these lines and the writings of Traherne, not to mention Vaughan ("The Retreate" and "Corruption"), poets whom Wordsworth certainly knew and who possessed some traits of the mystic.

ll. 51–2 *a Tree . . . A single Field.* The "tall ash" opposite his bedroom window at Hawkshead (*Prelude*, IV, *ll.* 86–92) and the "single tree" at Cambridge (*Prelude*, VI, *ll.* 76–94) may have been in his mind. The "single field" may have been "the one green field" described in *Poems on the Naming of Places*.

l. 85 *et seq. Behold the Child.* The child is Coleridge's son Hartley.

l. 103 *"humorous stage".* From the first line of a sonnet of Daniel.

ll. 109–20 Coleridge quotes these lines in his *Biographia Literaria* (Chapter XXII) as an example of "mental bombast or thoughts and images too great for the subject".

ll. 121–4 Wordsworth omitted these lines after his 1815 edition in deference to Coleridge's criticism (*Biographia Literaria*, Chapter XXII) that the notion of lying awake in the grave was a fearful one. Professor de Selincourt quotes an apt and illuminating passage from Dorothy's *Journal*: "We went to John's grave, sate a while at first. Afterwards William lay and I lay, in a trench under the fence—he with his eyes shut and listening to the waterfalls and the birds . . . we both lay still, and unseen by one another; he thought that it would be sweet thus to lie so in the grave, to hear the *peaceful* sounds of the earth, and just to know that our dear friends were near."

l. 185 *primal sympathy.* See *The Prelude*, I, *ll.* 555–8.

l. 206 *meanest flower.* An echo of Gray "The meanest floweret of the vale" from "Ode on the Pleasure arising from Vicissitude".

p. 176 BEGGARS. The composition of this poem illustrates Wordsworth's notion of "emotion recollected in tranquillity". Dorothy describes how a

beggar woman called at their door on Friday, 27 May 1800. Some
two years later (1802) Wordsworth wrote his poem on the subject.
The woman was "tall much beyond the measure of tall women. . . .
She had on a very long brown cloak and a very white cap, without
bonnet. Her face was excessively brown. . . ." Wordsworth took the
account from Dorothy. He did not meet the beggars—an interesting
example of the extraordinary collaboration between William and
Dorothy.

p. 178 I WANDERED LONELY AS A CLOUD. Wordsworth told Isabella Fenwick that
the two best lines (*ll.* 21 and 22) were by Mary. Composed in 1804 on
an experience recollected from 15 April 1802, and described in Dorothy's
Grasmere Journal thus: "We saw a few daffodils close to the waterside.
We fancied that the lake had floated the seeds ashore, and that the little
colony had so sprung up. But as we went along there were more and
yet more; and at last, under the boughs of the trees, we saw that there
was a long belt of them along the shore, about the breadth of a country
turnpike road. I never saw daffodils so beautiful. They grew among
the mossy stones about and about them; some rested their heads upon
these stones, as on a pillow, for weariness; and the rest tossed and reeled
and danced, and seemed as if they verily laughed with the wind, that
blew upon them over the lake; they looked so gay, ever glancing, ever
changing." These daffodils were in the woods beyond Gowbarrow
Park.

p. 179 THE SOLITARY REAPER. Dorothy mentions in her *Recollections of a Tour
made in Scotland* that this poem was suggested to Wordsworth by "a
beautiful sentence in Thomas Wilkinson's *Tour in Scotland*". The sentence is to be found in a commonplace book kept by Wordsworth. It
runs: "Passed by a Female who was reaping alone, she sung in Erse as
she bended over her sickle, the sweetest human voice I ever heard. Her
strains were tenderly melancholy, and felt delicious long after they were
heard no more."

p. 180 ELEGIAC STANZAS SUGGESTED BY A PICTURE OF PEELE CASTLE. This picture
painted by Sir George Beaumont reminded the poet of his brother John
and of his visit to Rampside in 1794. Rampside faces the promontory
on which Peele Castle stands in North Lancashire.

l. 36 *deep distress.* The death of his brother John.

l. 42 *Him whom I deplore.* His brother John.

p. 183 CHARACTER OF THE HAPPY WARRIOR. The poem was based on the poet's
brother John as well as on Nelson. One suspects that it is, in fact, an

idealized portrait of John and owes rather less to Nelson. In his note to Isabella Fenwick Wordsworth says: "... many elements of the character here portrayed were found in my brother John. ... His messmates used to call him the Philosopher, from which it must be inferred that the qualities and dispositions I allude to had not escaped their notice."

p. 186 ODE TO DUTY. Based on Gray's "Ode to Adversity", a poem written in the style of Horace. Milton's influence is much in evidence.

l. 1 *Daughter of the Voice of God!* echoes *Paradise Lost*, Book IX, *ll.* 652–3;

l. 54 *lowly wise*, echoes *Paradise Lost*, Book VIII, *l.* 173, "Be lowly wise". The poem has a fresh, unaffected moral strain. The poet's humility is clearly apparent.

The Prelude

Wordsworth seems to have conceived the idea of this poem in Germany in 1798, where he wrote portions of it. The selected passages come from both the version of 1805 and 1850, as shown.

p. 188 CHILDHOOD 1 (Book I, *ll.* 301–543, 1850 Text).

l. 2 *Fostered alike ... fear.* Compare Book XIV, *ll.* 244–6:
I too exclusively esteemed *that* love, And sought *that* beauty, which, as Milton sings, Hath terror in it.

l. 4 *that belovèd Vale.* Esthwaite, in which Hawkshead, the village of Wordsworth's schooldays, is situated.

l. 57 *et seq.* This episode occurred on Ullswater.

l. 77 *craggy steep.* Stybarrow Crag.

l. 78 *huge peak.* This peak is the Black Crag which comes into view as one rows out from the shore at a point near where Stybarrow touches the water.

ll. 158–63 Compare "There was a boy". We are in the essential climate of Wordsworth's poetry with these evocations of a boy's sense of the beyond.

l. 199 *et seq.* Like other pupils in the school at Hawkshead, Wordsworth boarded. He lived at the house of Anne Tyson (in all, for nine years).

l. 216 *Loo.* A round card game in which penalties are paid to the pool.

l. 243 *Bothnic Main.* Baltic Sea.

p. 195 CHILDHOOD 2 (Book II, *ll.* 138–418, 1850 Text).

ll. 1–3 The bay is Bowness and the tavern, the *White Lion*.

l. 31 *The Minstrel of the Troop.* Robert Greenwood, later Senior Fellow of Trinity College, Cambridge.

l. 60 *dear Vale.* Esthwaite.

l. 79 *false secondary power.* Analytic reason (see page 46 of Introduction, on *Godwinism*). Compared to intuition, analytic reason was, in Wordsworth's view, "secondary".

l. 158 *"best society".* See *Paradise Lost,* Book IX, *l.* 249.

l. 193 *the hours of school.* The school day at Hawkshead began at 6 a.m. in summer and 7 a.m. in winter.

l. 194 *little lake.* Esthwaite.

l. 196 *a Friend.* Probably the Rev. John Fleming, of Rayrigg, Windermere, though the Rev. Charles Farish has been mentioned by some editors.

p. 203 THE THEME (Book III, *ll.* 173–93, 1850 Text).

ll. 5–8 Professor de Selincourt points out that this was written in February 1804, about the time when Wordsworth finished the *Immortality Ode.*

p. 204 THE DISCHARGED SOLDIER (Book IV, *ll.* 370–469, 1850 Text). Professor de Selincourt observes that Wordsworth's meeting with the discharged soldier haunted his imagination, judging by evidence from the poet's notebooks. The story of the meeting was probably written early in 1798 and is therefore one of the first parts of *The Prelude.* There are resemblances to "The Old Cumberland Beggar", written at the same time.

p. 207 CROSSING THE ALPS (Book VI, *ll.* 523–648, 1850 Text).

l. 2 *bare ridge.* Probably the Col de Balme from which the view of Mont Blanc is certainly unimpressive.

l. 41 *rugged road.* 17 August 1790.

ll. 70–94 Professor de Selincourt's note on this passage is useful (see p. 559 of his edition of *The Prelude*). Among other things he says: "Wordsworth made many efforts to give a satisfactory philosophic account of the imagination. It was easier to him to say what it was not than what it was. It was a higher quality than fancy; it had nothing to do with the processes of the analytic reason, but rather seemed to have some relation with the affections and the moral nature. But his inability to understand or to define it did not affect his faith in its reality."

l. 123 *A dreary mansion.* This refers to the old hospice in the Simplon, situated beside a torrent below road level.

p. 210 THE FRENCH REVOLUTION I (Book X, *ll.* 236–99, 1850 Text).

l. 4 *Albion's shore.* Wordsworth left England in November 1791, and returned in December 1792.

l. 10 *the great City.* He remained in London from winter 1792 to spring 1793.

l. 14 *traffickers in Negro blood.* Clarkson and Wilberforce had founded the Society for the suppression of the slave trade in 1787.

l. 30 *confederate Powers.* France declared war on England and Holland 1 February 1793; England declared war on France on 11 February 1793.

l. 33 *et seq.* This important passage underlines the fact that Wordsworth's great moral shock arose from England's siding against the Revolution.

l. 51 *Englishmen by thousands . . . o'erthrown.* In September 1793 the Duke of York was defeated at Hondshoote.

p. 212 THE FRENCH REVOLUTION 2 (Book X, *ll.* 331–415, 1850 Text).

l. 3 *new enemy.* England.

l. 13 *God.* On 10 November 1793, an actress portraying the Goddess of Reason proceeded from the throne of Notre Dame to the Assembly where she sat beside the President. This was a kind of formal enthronement of Reason in Revolutionary Paris.

l. 26 *Domestic carnage.* The Reign of Terror lasting from 25 September 1793 to 26 July 1794, i.e. the period of Robespierre's ascendency.

l. 53 Madame Roland, guillotined on 8 November, 1793, exclaimed: "O liberté! que de crimes on commet en ton nom!"

p. 215 REJECTION OF REASON (Book X, *ll.* 663–941, 1805 Text). The passage opens with an account of matters already dealt with in Books IX and X. The parallel passage in 1850 text is Book XI, *ll.* 79–370.

l. 113 In a long and important note on the passage following this line, Professor de Selincourt observes that when Wordsworth talks of "wild theories" he refers to Godwinism. The meaning of the phrase "lent a careless ear" (*l.* 115) is that Wordsworth accepted those parts of Godwin's philosophy which did not run counter to the Revolution but that he did not grasp the full implications of Godwin's beliefs.

ll. 118–29 Wordsworth refers here to the doubts about the Revolution which grew in his mind as the Revolutionary Government ("events themselves") went to war, and to his search elsewhere for a more secure basis for his optimism about the Revolution. The search ended with his embracing Godwinism. Professor de Selincourt dates Wordsworth's change of faith in the outcome of the Revolution to Godwinism as the spring of 1795. He estimates that by September 1795 he had changed again, away from Godwinism. He estimates that Wordsworth took until 1797 (even with the help of Dorothy and Coleridge) to work through the disillusionment and despair that came over him once he had rejected Godwinism.

l. 130 *et seq.* As Professor de Selincourt observes, towards the end of 1794

Wordsworth recognized the French as "Oppressors". In September and October 1794 the French armies won victories in Holland, Italy, and Spain.

l. 157 *et seq.* The "delight" lies in the discovery he mistakenly supposed he had made that the "individual mind", basing itself upon reason, is the supreme arbiter. Very similar ideas occur in *The Borderers, ll.* 1493–6.

ll. 207–8 *two natures . . . melancholy.* This passage, to be found only in the 1805 text, suggests that Wordsworth had a temperamental leaning towards melancholy. If true, this would partly explain why he succumbed so completely (albeit briefly) to Godwinism. His letters contain numerous references to ill-health.

l. 242 *Turn'd towards mathematics.* Mathematics provided him with a sense of security after his rejection of Godwinism.

l. 244 *most precious Friend!* Refers to Coleridge, whose influence followed Dorothy's.

l. 248 *Those days.* He joined Dorothy in Halifax in 1794. Both longed to be together.

ll. 271–2 Napoleon summoned the Pope to anoint him Emperor of the French in 1804.

p. 223 NATURE'S STRENGTH (Book XI, *ll.* 138–343, 1805 Text). The parallel passage in the 1850 text is Book XII, *ll.* 93–286. Here Wordsworth presents his idea of Nature as a source of spiritual strength.

ll. 36–9 This dominance of sense-impression occurred at two particular stages of Wordsworth's life, in youth (the time of "dizzy raptures") and after the war with France (spring 1793) had produced his first moral crisis. It appears to have blocked the way to his deepest mystic experience.

l. 62 *a Maid.* Mary Hutchinson, his wife.

ll. 97–8 Here he writes of feelings arising naturally from sense-impressions. The text of 1850 speaks here of "piety" as an "eternal sanction" (to quote Professor de Selincourt), supported by reflection: "I felt, observed, and pondered."

The 1805 version expresses Wordsworth's original meaning.

ll. 142–79 This incident took place at Cowdrake Quarry on the Edenhall side of Penrith Beacon. Thomas Parker was murdered here on 18 November 1766, by Thomas Nicholson who was executed near the scene of the murder on 31 August 1767.

l. 146 *honest James.* Servant to Wordsworth's father.

l. 180 *two dear Ones.* Omitted from the 1850 version. The reference is to Dorothy and Mary. In Book VI, line 245 echoes line 180 here, "The spirit of pleasure and youth's golden gleam". The Book VI passage describes the visit to this place (the Border Beacon, near Penrith). A comparison of the passages in each book (VI and XI (1805)) suggests the idea that Mary Hutchinson could have been Wordsworth's first love, the inspiration of the *Lucy* poems, only temporarily displaced by Annette Vallon.

p. 229 THE IMAGINATION (Book XIV, *ll.* 11–301, 1850 Text). For Wordsworth this passage is the climax of the poem. The 1850 version is rather better, as poetry, than that of 1805, but one or two lines fall below the earlier version. The parallel passage in 1805 is Book XIII, *ll.* 10–268.

Wordsworth explores the nature and function of the imagination and of the creative mind. Professor de Selincourt writes: "In his reflections that arose from the scene on Snowdon, Wordsworth follows two lines of thought: first, the function of the human imagination; and secondly, beyond and beneath this, the essential character and activity, no less spiritual than intellectual, of the 'higher mind' itself." (*The Prelude*, ed. de Selincourt, edition of 1959 revised by Helen Darbishire, p. 619.) In writing again of his experience as a mystic Wordsworth suggests that his sense of the cosmic energy became a thought:

> The feeling of life endless, the great thought
> By which we live, Infinity and God
> XIII, ll. 183–4, 1805 (XIV, ll. 204–5, 1850)

Professor de Selincourt has compared various "try-out" passages for this section of the poem (XIII, *ll.* 66–106, 1805) from which he deduces that Wordsworth attempted "to define the experience and the qualities essential to the poet: lively sensuous experience comes first; imaginative use of that experience comes next; spiritual insight of the deepest and purest kind in the centre (for Wordsworth this is clearly the experience of the mystic); but the rational and moral basis of the poet's thought is also insisted upon: he must 'bend to general laws'—he must be a 'professed servant of the Truth'."

ll. 171–7 The 1805 version of these lines clearly represents love as an integral part of man and not as dependent on Christian faith. The text of 1850 obscures the poet's original intention by covering over the meaning with Christian words.

l. 194 Again the 1850 version conceals the original sense of 1805 under Christian phrasing. The 1805 lines are XIII, *ll.* 183–4, quoted at the beginning of the notes on this section.

ll. 256–65 These nine lines do not occur in the 1805 version. They suggest, erroneously, that the poet's wife, Mary Hutchinson, played an important part in this development up to 1798.

l. 265 *et seq.* A generous and warmhearted tribute to Coleridge whose influence upon him was immensely important. Coleridge helped him to understand his aims as a poet. Later he said of Coleridge: "He was most wonderful in the power he possessed of throwing out in profusion grand central truths from which might be evolved the most comprehensive systems."

INDEX OF FIRST LINES

A slumber did my spirit seal   *page* 126
Before I see another day   116
Behold her, single in the field   179
Earth has not anything to show more fair   160
Fair seed-time had my soul, and I grew up   188
Five years have past; five summers, with the length   104
Her eyes are wild, her head is bare   113
I had approach'd, like other Youth, the Shield   215
I hate that Andrew Jones: he'll breed   150
I saw an aged Beggar in my walk   80
I thought of Thee, my partner and my guide   162
I travelled among unknown men   124
I wandered lonely as a cloud   178
I was thy neighbour once, thou rugged Pile   180
If from the public way you turn your steps   136
In distant countries have I been   109
In France, the men, who, for their desperate ends   212
In the sweet shire of Cardigan   86
It is a beauteous evening, calm and free   161
It seems a day   119
It was a close, warm, breezeless summer night   229
Midway on long Winander's eastern shore   195
Milton! thou shouldst be living at this hour   163
Not of outward things   203
Nuns fret not at their convent's narrow room   161
O blithe New-comer! I have heard   166
Oh! soul of Nature, excellent and fair   223
Once, when those summer months   204
One morning (raw it was and wet   167
She dwelt among the untrodden ways   124

She had a tall man's height or more   *page* 176
Stern Daughter of the Voice of God   186
Strange fits of passion have I known   123
Supine the Wanderer lay   65
Surprised by joy—impatient as the Wind   162
That very day   207
The Cock is crowing   168
The post-boy drove with fierce career   163
There was a Boy; ye knew him well, ye cliffs   121
There was a roaring in the wind all night   155
There was a time when meadow, grove, and stream   169
The world is too much with us; late and soon   161
Three years she grew in sun and shower   125
'Tis eight o'clock,—a clear March night   89
Twice had the trees let fall   210
When Ruth was left half desolate   127
Where art thou, my beloved Son   152
Who is the happy Warrior? Who is he   183